TUNES FROM A TUSCAN GUITAR

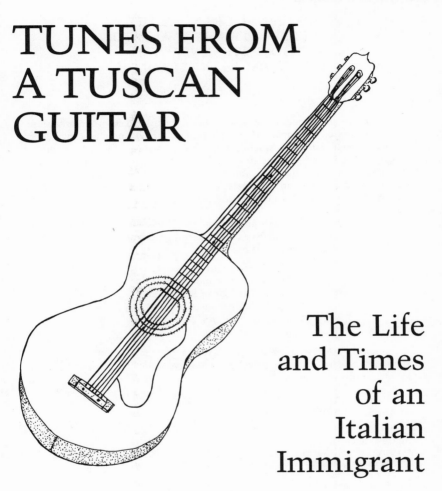

The Life
and Times
of an
Italian
Immigrant

Roland R. Bianchi

Fithian Press • Santa Barbara • 1994

THIS BOOK IS DEDICATED
TO THE MEMORY OF MY
PATERNAL GRANDFATHER,
OTTORINO BIANCHI, AND TO
THOSE WHO KNEW AND
LOVED HIM AS MUCH AS I DID.

R.R.B.

I cannot authenticate all the persons, places, events and dates herein because this story is based on hearsay. My grandfather was articulate in relating his experiences about coming to America. From my conversations with him while I was growing up, I have selected stories corroborated by friends and relatives, and compiled what I knew about my grandfather firsthand. Any similarities between characters, their names and occupations, and those of people now deceased or presently alive is purely accidental and coincidental.

The following individuals graciously offered technical, grammatical and historical assistance. I am indebted to their contributions and help for the refinement of the initial drafts of this book.

Mrs. Petey Grant
Mrs. Lorraine Guidi Rinaldi
Mrs. Carol Martin Schuettge
Mr. Richard Schuettge
Mrs. Lee Moriarty
Mrs. Alice Kleeman

I especially extend a heartfelt thank-you to my wife, Judy, and our friends Sue and Reg Hearn, who encouraged me to preserve stories about my grandfather for my family and friends.

Published by Fithian Press
A division of Daniel and Daniel, Publishers, Inc.
Post Office Box 1525
Santa Barbara, CA 93102

Library of Congress cataloging-in-publication data
Bianchi, Roland R.
    Tunes from a Tuscan guitar : the life and times of an Italian immigrant / Roland R. Bianchi
        p.   cm
    ISBN 1-56474-085-4
    1. Bianchi, Ottorino, 1903–   . 2. Italian Americans—California—San Francisco—Biography. 3. Fishers—California—San Francisco—Biography. 4. San Francisco (Calif.)—Biography. I. Title.
    F869.S39I816   1994
    979.4'6100451'092—dc20
        [B]   93-39878
                                                        CIP

CONTENTS

Tunes from a Tuscan Guitar

Bianchi-Guidi Family
1952

Ottorino
Elisa

Renato (son)	Renata (daughter)
Beatrice (spouse)	Guido (spouse)

Roland (son) Ray (son)　　Lorraine　　Jean
(author)　　　　　　　(daughter)　(daughter)

Back Row:
Beatrice Campi Bianchi, Roland R. Bianchi,
Lorraine Rinaldi (née Guidi), Guido Guidi
Front Row:
Ray Robert Bianchi, Renato Bianchi,
Elisa Guerrazzi Bianchi, Ottorino Bianchi,
Renata Bianchi Guidi, Jean Winter (née Guidi)

Introduction

Above all else, he loved children, his own, his grand-children, and anybody's little kids he happened to meet. He loved me.

He was a merciless tease to little boys and girls alike, and he went out of his way to play harmless pranks on them just to experience their reactions. With equal patience, he would make them toys or articles of amusement and could sit them on his knee astounding their imagination with countless marvelous stories—each instinctively suited to the child's temperament or maturity. He was a good storyteller, a Renaissance man of practical wisdom and natural skills and creativity which he felt duty-bound to share with anyone who would listen and some who would not. Nonno Ottorino was a character of incessant jest, keen sense of humor and a lust for the artistic, the literary and scholastic things in life. And though he never had a formal education, he was so well read, and had such a phenomenal memory, he could recall entire poems or passages from the classics or literature of his day. He influenced and enriched my childhood more than any other individual in my life.

He even looked like the kindly grandfather in everybody's fantasies. A once-aquiline nose, broken in a fall during childhood, became a mushroom pug enhancing a ruddy countenance. But for the long beard, he was the spitting image of Santa Claus—down to a full white mustache, twinkling blue eyes and a homemade pipe permanently grafted to the corner of his mouth.

His image, in my memory, always included his battered heavy felt hat. Rarely did it rest as intended. Invariably, it sat askance on the back of his head, about 45 degrees off plumb. It always revealed his mood of the moment, serious if worn forward, which was infrequent, convivial if smashed upon his crown out of instinct without regard to any alignment. The task or situation at hand always dictated how he would unconsciously position his hat, and it always made me laugh.

Because of his intellectual avocation, you would not have expected Ottorino Bianchi to become a commercial fisherman, and indeed, he did not do so by choice. Nevertheless, he brought a grace and pride to that profession that later earned him the recognition of his peers. He stood out in stark contrast to the illiteracy and poverty predominant among his co-workers on the San Francisco Fisherman's Wharf in the early 1900s. How he got there is what this story is about. The story begins in Bientina, Italy, a small town northeast of Pisa, amid the amber tones of the Tuscan countryside.

1

Bientina

Bientina had the dubious history of having been a penal colony because it was situated in a swamp. Law-breakers were isolated there during the Renaissance, and presumably the modern Bientinesi inherited an inbred legacy that accounted for their propensity to be quick-tempered, tenacious, freedom-loving and libertine. Of course, this was a myth, but Bientinesi to this day are proud of their background and espouse whichever characteristics suit their egos. Among other Pisani, the reputation of the Bientinesi was that you gave them a wide berth and avoided them socially, if possible.

The swamp had long been reclaimed into beautiful fields for grains, vineyards and olive and chestnut orchards when Ottorino was born and grew up on lands near Bientina owned by the Guerrazzis, landed gentry who could prove their lineage back to the Roman Senate.

Ottorino had an older sister named Santina and two younger brothers named Silvio and Tonino. They were children of a contadino (resident farmer). His parents were resident farmers who tended to the Guerrazzi estate in return for crop shares and housing. The arrangement was not unlike the manor-serf institution that grew out of medieval England.

My great-grandmother, Fulvia, was determined her children should aspire to more than *contadini* and working other people's land. She had learned to read and she held classes for her children each morning to teach them this skill. She tutored her children in the basics of math, and further, instilled the love of art and music, because

3

she craved these values for herself. Ottorino took to this book learning like a duck to water. He became a ravenous reader, utilizing the private library of the Guerrazzi household, to which his mother had access.

Encouraged by his mother, Ottorino learned to play the guitar, first by ear, but later by studying music and memorizing all the chords by name and function in any key. As a result, he was sought after for parties to accompany any other instrumentalists or vocalists. He sang *stornelli* (folk songs) and became popular with the social set as an accomplished musician and raconteur of literature who impressed the local scholars attending the university in nearby Pisa.

Though dedicated to helping his father and siblings on the podere, the land assigned to be cultivated, Ottorino's reputation as a fun-loving "bon vivant" did not escape the attention of Guerrazzi's eldest daughter, Elisa. Her sisters and brothers scoffed at Elisa's attention to Ottorino as being beneath her social station in life. But it became more than coincidence that the Guerrazzis' social entertaining always seemed to include their local "troubadour," Ottorino.

Forbidden love and marrying outside one's station were no different in Tuscany than anywhere else, and the potential for contempt and family rejection no less. Elisa fell hopelessly in love with Ottorino, and she risked being ostracized by her family for having the audacity to become the bride of Aurelio Ottorino Del Bianco.[1]

---

[1]Original marriage and birth records conflict and interchangeably refer to Del Bianco and to Bianchi as the proper surname. This dichotomy provided some consternation at Ellis Island, as we shall see in Chapter IV.

4

Elisa moved in with her in-laws to be away from the criticism in the Guerrazzi manor, and she and Ottorino had Renato, their first-born son, who became my father.

There was a depression in Europe in 1903 when my dad was born. The Guerrazzi family cut back arable acreage and let many servants go. Ottorino saw he would have difficulty supporting his bride and child. He had heard of work in the shipyards of France near Le Havre, and he left his new family to seek employment there. According to Nonno, the French Basques held the majority of good-paying jobs in the shipyards. He described the Basques as a clannish bunch, jealous of their women and prejudiced against everyone, including the French. The small contingent of Italian job seekers fared poorly, and indeed had it not been for Ottorino's talent as a musician, he might have starved.

After six months, Ottorino returned home dejected and just as poor. Elisa informed him that in his absence, his sister Santina had run away to America with her boyfriend, a "ne'er-do-well" named Pellegrini. Though the neighbors wrote off Santina for her arrogance and for flaunting her Bientinese trait of "independence," Ottorino kept up a correspondence with her because he cared about his older sister and her welfare. This correspondence gave Ottorino the first glimpse of America's promise.

2

Departure

"Dear *Soscio*," began one of Santina's letters, "America is vast . . . Love, Santina." *Soscio* (pronounced Shawshow), was the nickname Santina had given her brother Ottorino. It's a name you would give to a kindly, big, St. Bernard dog. Anybody who took life the way it came was a *soscio*, and it suited Ottorino as a child. Santina didn't spare her other brothers; she called Silvio "La-La." It connoted compliance and reservation. Silvio later emigrated to become a successful farmer in Santa Clara, California. The third brother, Tonino, she called *Naudo* (literally, a knot). Tonino was intense, rigid, had a violent temper and constantly left home on mercenary campaigns. We believe he died in the Abyssinian War — a "libertine" Bientinese to the end.

"Dear Santina, It's so hard to find work. Today's meal consisted of one *salachino* (salted herring) for six people. We all dunked bread in the oil of the fish as it was passed around — then gave the remnant of smashed meat to Renato, as he is the youngest. Love, *Soscio*."

"Dear *Soscio*, This country is so big. It's growing. You can find work here. Pellegrini and I are struggling in San Francisco, but we eat. Bring your guitar. Love, Santina."

"Dear Santina, If I come to America, how long will it be before I can send for Elisa and Renato?"

"Dear Ottorino, I don't know, but you are welcome to stay with Pellegrini and me for a short while until you decide to stay or go back. It may get crowded — I am pregnant."

7

"Dear Santina, Elisa and I talked it over—I have no choice. The minute I can accumulate the fare, I must come to America. I told Elisa, 'Since an Italian discovered it and since it was named after an Italian, it couldn't be all that bad!'"

It had to be a wrenching experience to leave a young child and wife. The guilt and doubts were not eased when Ottorino arrived in Le Havre, France, to await departure. He chose Le Havre as opposed to Naples or other Mediterranean ports because of the contacts he had made while working in France. The passage from Naples to New York cost almost twice as much as from Le Havre, France. This was because Le Havre was the last port of call before New York for the *Bretagna*. Staying with friends in Le Havre permitted the equivalent of today's "standby" fare for steerage class.

At dockside, there was gloom and sadness among those waiting to leave on debarkation day. The crying of those who could not go, but who were there to see their loved ones off, was demoralizing to Ottorino. How lucky, he thought, for those who could travel as a family. He was glad that he had said goodbye to Elisa and Renato in Bientina. He thanked his acquaintances who housed him and had come to see him leave. He boarded the steamship *Bretagna* in January of 1906.

The many rust stains from the rivets in the steel plates of the hull bled through the black paint and didn't impart great confidence in the seaworthiness of the vessel about to make a winter crossing of the North Atlantic. This premonition of doom didn't disappear when Ottorino was ushered to steerage.

Steerage was the cheapest travel class and Ottorino expected spartan accommodations, but he wasn't prepared for his assigned quarters. Beneath the water line and at the stern of the vessel, in a space no bigger than 8 by 10 feet, were three stacked bunks bolted to the hull's steel plates, slanting toward the keel at a precipitous angle. The flat rusty floor space was close to 3 by 6 feet. There was a permanently sealed porthole near the top bunk, as it was under water when the ship was fully loaded. A grate serving as a partition was opposite the bunks, through which you could look down to the drive shaft of the starboard propeller. Its lubrication made it glisten, but the stench of machine oil and lead paint was oppressive. Through the opposite grate on the other side of the drive shaft, Ottorino could see stacks of salted, stiff, green animal hides. It was obvious that they had been riding the seas a long time. They smelled of rancid fat. Much to Ottorino's amazement, there were passengers amid the hides attempting to stake out living space. Suitcases and trunks were jammed between the stacks. One man had spread a blanket on top of some hides and he was lying there, apparently resting or asleep.

The *Bretagna* had come from Malta by way of Naples and then north to the west coast of France. Ottorino could detect Arabic, Maltese, French and Sicilian dialects as his co-passengers tried to make themselves comfortable. He clambered for the top bunk to be near the porthole. There was a suitcase there, which he removed to the next bunk below. His carry-on effects were a drawstring sack and his guitar. He used the sack as a pillow and placed the guitar between himself and the bulkhead. He stared at a maze of steam pipes not more than a foot above his face. Back toward the companionway from which he had come was a single bathroom. It served both compartments on either side of the propeller shaft. Ottorino counted six men, two women and two children, including the man asleep on the hides.

Ottorino was terrified by the thought of the ship taking on water. Surely he would drown, for a locked gate through which he came down the steel stairwell was well below the waterline. He could only occasionally see daylight through his porthole as the ship rocked with the swells at dockside.

The claustrophobic feeling was about to send him protesting, when he heard the blast of the smokestack that reverberated throughout the ship. A metal-on-metal clunk engaged the propeller shaft with a bang, and the noise of churning propeller blades confirmed they were just outside the bulkhead of his bunk. The journey to America had begun, and Ottorino wondered how he could ever survive the noise and the lack of fresh air that was already irritating his eyes.

※ ※ ※

A Filipino steward unceremoniously dumped a dozen or so life jackets and mattress covers at the foot of the stairwell. He was barking instructions in English, but no one understood him. Ottorino was fascinated, for he had never seen a Filipino. At first he thought he was Chinese.

"What do you think he said?" said Ottorino out loud. He was grateful one of the Sicilian passengers acknowledged his question.

"We're supposed to take a life saver and mattress cover," said the Sicilian. "Can I use the lower bunk on your side?"

"Of course," said Ottorino. He was happy he could converse with someone, even through the difficulties of the dialect.

"Whose suitcase on the second bunk?" asked the Sicilian.

"I don't know," said Ottorino.

"I'd like my children to sleep there," said the Sicilian.

That's when Ottorino learned that Dominic Battaglia and his wife and two children were headed for Erie, Pa. (Dominic pronounced it phonetically as one word, "Eriepah.")

Dominic's children were named Lupo and Teresa. Lupo was a boy of about five. His sister, Teresa, was perhaps seven years old. Both children had the darkest black, penetrating eyes Ottorino had ever seen. As the children were told by their father to bring their belongings to the middle bunk, Ottorino picked up his guitar and strummed a few choruses of "Ochi Neri" (Black Eyes), a popular Italian song. Dominic grinned as he saw the humor in the gesture—and called to his wife, "Come meet compadre Bianchi." A short, robust lady in dark clothes crossed the propeller shaft through the passageway connecting the two compartments. She smiled at Ottorino, who was still singing "Ochi Neri," and by this time the children had joined in the chorus.

"Don't you bother this nice man," said Mrs. Battaglia. The children stopped singing while Mr. and Mrs. Battaglia whispered to each other. Ottorino suspected they were trying to decide who would take the lower bunk. It turned out Lupo and his dad stayed on Ottorino's side. Mrs. Battaglia and Teresa returned to the other compartment to be with the only other lady Ottorino had seen.

The passengers began covering their bunk pads with the mattress covers—all except the man sleeping on the hides. Ottorino grabbed an extra unclaimed mattress cover to use to protect his guitar. He worried about the condensation of moisture forming on the bulkheads. If you ran your finger on the steel plates, water droplets ran down. While he was playing "Ochi Neri" for the Battaglia children, he could tell his guitar was already out of tune.

Ottorino wondered what time it was. The ship was to have left at 3:00 p.m. with the outgoing tide, and he estimated they had been under way about an hour. He went to the other side of the propeller shaft where the hides were stacked to learn who else was there and if anyone knew the time. He pointed to his wrist as he made eye contact with some of the Arab and French passengers. The only other lady, whom he later found out was Maltese, searched through some belongings and pulled out a watch. It was 4:30. He also pointed to the man sleeping on the hides. Everyone shrugged their shoulders. It was obvious he was traveling alone.

Ottorino was getting hungry, as he had skipped lunch. He wondered what feeding regimen people in steerage were afforded. He knew he had some hardtack cheese, salami and a can of sardines that Elisa had packed in his sack. But these were emergency rations and he couldn't see resorting to them just an hour and a half out of Le Havre. The thought of 14 days in this environment depressed him.

He returned to his bunk after a cursory examination of the toilet facilities—one sink or basin, one faucet (cold), one toilet with continuous running sea water. Ottorino's sense of humor got the best of him when he saw the toilet. "Such luxury," he mused, "you don't even have to flush." He returned to his bunk and decided he had better protect his valuables and currency. Taking his pocket knife, he bored a hole through the corner of his passport. He pulled a cotton drawstring from the spare mattress cover and threaded the hole to create a necklace. In the passport pocket, he placed a $5.00 U.S. greenback that Santina had sent him, his Italian *lire* (maybe $200 U.S. dollars' worth), and Santina's S.F. address, along with a spare passport picture she had sent him weeks before. He carried these items, along with the ship's boarding pass and railroad ticket, around his neck and under his shirt. Satisfied these valuables were safe on his person, he lay back to stare at the intricacies of the steam pipes above his head. Soon the gentle motion of the *Bretagna* made him forget he was hungry, and it lulled him to sleep.

3

The Crossing

"Signore Bianchi, wake up," said Lupo. Startled and disoriented from a deep sleep, Ottorino sat up and bumped his forehead on the nearest steam pipe. He couldn't decide what was worse—the smell of food, the gurgling of his empty stomach or the pain he received from the bump. Lupo laughed at the reaction he caused by waking up Ottorino. "Don't you ever do that again," Ottorino said crossly; then realizing the boy was alerting him for dinner, he felt bad and apologized.

The same Filipino steward had delivered some covered dishes, assorted fruit and dessert. The smell was getting better from the dishes—some kind of stew over soggy, overcooked rice.

"How long did I sleep?" asked Ottorino. Mr. Battaglia said it was eight o'clock. "I think we got a problem," said Battaglia. "The man on the hides appears feverish. We tried to rouse him when the food came, but he refused to move."

Ottorino reached for his covered stew and grabbed a remaining orange. He noticed Teresa had an orange but not Lupo, who was attacking his stew. All the stories about scurvy flashed across Ottorino's mind, but he sacrificed his orange and gave it to Lupo. The dessert tray had leftover pieces of cake on it. It was obvious the cake had been salvaged from what first-class passengers had not eaten. In some cases the fork imprints were still in the frosting.

The meal was quickly and silently devoured by everybody. The remaining covered dish intended for the sick man on the hides sat there tempting the unsatiated appetites. It didn't stay there long. One of the Arabs circulated about with nine toothpicks fanned out between the first and second fingers of his clenched fist. Everyone was invited to pluck a toothpick. Ottorino was glad that the short toothpick was pulled by Teresa. She shared her prize with her mother and brother. Dominic rejected his family's offer for extra food and became more concerned about the sick man who had forfeited his first meal en route to America.

"If he is seriously ill," said Dominic, "we can all become infected in these tight quarters." He was worrying about his children, more than himself.

"If he's not better by morning," said Ottorino, "we'll have to call the steward. It's best we leave him alone."

Suddenly the only lights in the compartment went out except for a small red bulb in a protected cage fixture. It was too dark to read—one could barely see. Though there was no explanation, everyone assumed this was a bedtime signal. The Maltese lady's watch indicated 9:30.

Mrs. Battaglia led her children to the bathroom. Others lined up in turn. The passengers sought out their territories to settle in for the night.

"I wonder if they will let us on deck tomorrow," thought Ottorino, as he removed his shoes and curled up on his bunk. The distraction of the meal made him forget the confinement. Then he reasoned that as a Bientinese, he should have inherited some tolerance for imprisonment.

A foul odor awakened Ottorino. It was still dark in the compartment, save for the red light. He speculated someone had gotten sick from the stew but the bathroom was vacant. He got down from his bunk, trying not to awaken Lupo and Dominic, but the latter stirred and said, "What's happening?"

"I don't know," whispered Ottorino, "but something is wrong." Both men instinctively looked over to the man on the hides. He hadn't changed position. On closer examination, both men simultaneously exclaimed, "E morto!" ("He's dead!").

A trickle of blood from the victim's mouth had coagulated on the fur of the hide. Body controls failed prior to death and accounted for the foul odor. The Maltese lady screeched upon realizing what had happened, and the entire compartment awoke to chaos. "Don't touch anything," admonished Mrs. Battaglia to her children. Ottorino went to the stairwell and pounded on the steel grate, yelling, "*Aiuto, aiuto!*" (Help, Help!).

The cabin lights came on and the Filipino steward descended the stairwell, half dressed, and understandably disturbed at the commotion. When he saw the passengers pointing to the corpse, he paled.

In the next twenty minutes, more people came and went from the crowded, cramped quarters until what appeared to be a medic or doctor covered the body. Someone said, "Step aside. It's the captain." Indeed, a fully uniformed gentleman dressed in blue with gold braid on his cap came to inspect the situation. It was obvious the captain was not pleased with what he found. The next order from the Filipino steward was, "Let's go, everybody top side." Ottorino didn't understand, but the steward's finger pointing upward was clear enough.

The early morning sea air was a welcome relief, and Ottorino breathed as heavily as he could to get the stench of his compartment out of his nostrils. The group gathered on the first deck, maybe twenty feet above the water. There was still another deck above before the main deck and superstructure. Ottorino tried to remember the stairwell and exits taken in case he ever had to leave steerage again. It felt so good to be outside. The stars of the English Channel were fading in the rays of dawn.

* * *

Squinting at the northern horizon, Ottorino could see land; he speculated it must be England. Lupo and Teresa started to complain they were cold, and the small group echoed their sentiments by jogging in place on the wet deck with arms crossed to protect numbing fingers. In the anxiety to leave steerage, few had time to take along coats or jackets. The initial exhilaration of fresh air now had noses running and exhaled breath condensed in puffs as people spoke.

The Filipino steward appeared again and made what Ottorino thought to be a long speech. The tone sounded apologetic. He motioned to be followed and everyone thought they were returning to their quarters. Instead, they were led to the third-class dining room. There were actual chairs and tables there. The room was empty except for cooks and crew setting up for the breakfast meal. The group was invited to two tables, and Ottorino recounted in later years that he would never forget the greatest breakfast of his life. Hot cereal, eggs, sausage, rolls, coffee—the works. He speculated with Dominic and his wife that the captain must have had some guilty feelings about the death in steerage and the unsanitary conditions among the hides. Everyone ate their fill. As they were escorted out by the Filipino steward, they waved and smiled at the cooks to show their appreciation for the surprise treatment.

They were further surprised when they got back down to their compartment. The hides were gone and a pungent odor of disinfectant permeated the compartment. There was no doubt somebody had ordered steerage to be scoured. Every surface had been wiped.

The Filipino's attitude of indifference had changed remarkably. He was smiling now and placing towels and pillows on each bunk. When he saw Ottorino's guitar, he mimicked strumming. How strange, thought Ottorino—though he was in the same hellhole he had entered the day before, the display of charity and concern and the attempt at cleanliness made such a difference. The hearty breakfast also had put everyone in a good mood, thanks to an unknown passenger who had the temerity to die. Ottorino had a twinge of misgiving about this good fortune. He felt bad that he had told Dominic to "wait 'til morning" about the sick man. Had they acted the night before, the passenger might still be alive. They never found out who the dead man was or why he died. But they were about to learn something, if the Arab with the toothpicks had his way.

The dead man's suitcase, which had been moved about—first by Ottorino and then by Dominic—had been placed in a corner by the clean-up crew. The Arab had the suitcase in one hand while the other sported nine toothpicks. It was raffle time again. But this time, Ottorino was offended. The dignity of the man's death, which had brought them some preferential treatment, should not be belittled this way. He likened the situation to that of the Roman soldiers at the crucifixion. Ottorino shook his head, "no," while staring at the Arab eyeball to eyeball. With his left hand he reached for the suitcase and with his right he enveloped the Arab's fist, crushing all the toothpicks. They stood that way for a moment while the remaining passengers froze in silence, expecting the worst from the confrontation. Gently but firmly, Ottorino jerked the suitcase free and backed away. Without losing eye contact with the Arab, he yelled to Dominic to call the steward. Moments later the steward arrived. Ottorino presented the suitcase to the steward. "Please, somebody tell him this belonged to the dead man."

To everybody's surprise, the Arab that Ottorino had challenged rattled something in fluent English — at least fluent enough for the steward to respond in gratitude and then to thank everyone else. Ottorino and the Arab smiled and shook hands.

Prospects for this trip turning into a pleasant one were looking better. The gate in the stairwell remained unlocked. Emile, the Filipino steward (he now wore his nameplate), was apparently under orders to see to their comfort. The dessert trays contained more fruit and full slices of cake. It was as if the passengers in the steerage compartment were blackmailing the management of the ship for the passenger's death. And the management was paying off.

✳ ✳ ✳

No one had to tell the passengers they were passing the Bay of Biscay. The *Bretagna* began to pitch the instant it cleared the Channel Islands. According to Ottorino, the incidence of pitch and roll increased daily as the vengeance of the North Atlantic whipped up 30-foot swells, as it is wont to do in early January.

Passengers were relegated to their cabins in all classes of travel, either out of fear or seasickness. More and more, Emile's covered dinner plates went begging at meal time. There was no chance the Arab with the toothpicks could raffle them off.

Just trying to stand up became a challenge as the vessel yawed with the running seas. When the bow descended into a wave trough, the propellers would spin audibly out of the water, shuddering the steerage compartment with vibrations expected to shatter the hull. The passengers prayed the bow would be permitted to rise, as it struggled against tons of water surging across the main deck. Once the bow was free, the stern groaned as the propellers found resistance again until the next elevator plunge buried the bow into the next wave. The compartment toilet had to be shut down because the water from the bowl splashed about the companionway.

Ottorino lay on his bunk on his back, embracing a steam pipe to keep from being tossed to the deck. He felt more seasick in an upright position, but on his back and hugging an insulated warm pipe was comforting. He was hungry, but reasoned he could not cope with the seasickness going on around him. Lupo and Teresa were crying between dry heaves. Others were up and down the stairwell vomiting over the side. Ottorino thought he would die, and then worried he would not. You get that desperate when you are seasick.[2]

Day and night blended into one another the rest of the voyage. Ottorino remembered at one point he

---

[2]His lesson of coping on his back while hanging onto a steam pipe came to my rescue when I was on a troop ship en route to Korea in 1952. The USS *Miegs*, with 5000 army personnel aboard met a rare Pacific storm. I survived on a top bunk on my back, hugging pipes above my head. I thought about Nonno all the way to Korea. I was sick, but not as scared as I might have been because my grandfather had told me what it was like.

hadn't smoked his pipe since departing. He took his tobacco and matches on deck one morning when he realized the seas had subsided. He had a hard time lighting his pipe, cupping the match flame from the wind—but after a few puffs, he began to feel human again. People on the upper decks were pointing off the starboard bow. Ottorino waved away his last puff of smoke to get a clearer look. Sure enough, the New York skyline was coming into view. With mouth agape, he stared and let his emotions bring tears to his eyes, though he didn't really know why. His pipe went out and he didn't bother to relight it. In a fleeting thought he recited Dante's quote to the entrance of hell: "Abandon hope all ye who enter." Then he chastised himself for such a pessimistic thought. "I've been through hell—this is America!"

Intent on watching the harbor tugs take their positions around the *Bretagna*, Ottorino missed a close-up view of the Statue of Liberty. "What you mean, you didn't see it?" said Dominic indignantly. "She is a-standing right there! Just like the Virgin Mary!"

Nonno (Grandpa) chuckled at Dominic's enthusiasm, and he understood it because Dominic and his family had weathered the Atlantic and a new life was waiting for them in "Eriepah." Ottorino still had miles and uncertainties to overcome, not the least of which was Ellis Island.

4

Ellis Island
and the Southern Route

Cages, wooden benches, and rumors. Mostly rumors. Not knowing if you were in the right line. Delays. Medical exams. Rumors they would send you back. Frustration. Multilingual signs, dated, obsolete and useless. Fear of quarantine. Fear of inoculations. Relinquishing passports without explanation. Separation of sexes in caged, drafty holding pens. Not knowing when or if you would be reunited with family, let alone luggage. Rumors you could bribe the guards. Rumors that if you did, they could send you back. Rip-offs. Customs inspections. Interrogations about sponsors. Errors on documents and especially inconsistencies regarding names and proper spelling. Were you "fit to land"? Ellis Island was a zoo.

When Ottorino saw Emile for the last time, the steward was placing a yellow tag over the head of each passenger as they stepped off the gangplank. Ottorino could only decipher the numbers on his tag, which he didn't know were matched to a manifest. There were other passengers with blue, red, and green tags. Customs officials holding megaphones waved colored cards corresponding to those worn by the passengers. Interpreters repeatedly shouted the message: "Step over here if you are wearing this card," and they said this in German, English, French, Italian, Spanish and Arabic. Ottorino worried about the Maltese lady understanding these directions, but she had joined the Battaglia family. It was apparent there were more yellow tags than any other color, as the passengers grouped before their respective official. A group at a time, they were escorted into the main building. The first order of business was running the medical gauntlet, the least of the indignities that were to follow. Fear itself became the biggest indignity of all.

Ottorino had been reunited with his sea trunk on the ferry from the *Bretagna* to Ellis Island. He now had to leave with his guitar and other stuff as he was directed through a maze of inspection stations. The most dreaded rumor was that they turned back your eyelids. It sounded like it would hurt. The doctors were looking for trachoma, a disease that could lead to blindness. In reality, the examination was harmless, but the fear wasn't. Nonno trudged past the next series of stations, then back to the main room with the baggage. Customs was next, and this took hours. An interpreter asked routine questions, while a seated officer went through every piece of baggage. They immediately confiscated Nonno's hardtack, cheese and salami. "No food," said the interpreter. They didn't touch the can of sardines. Nonno didn't protest, but how he wished he had eaten the cheese and salami at sea.

Ottorino saw Dominic back in the line, but not Mrs. Battaglia. "Where's your family?" shouted Ottorino.

"I don't know," said Dominic, very worried. "We were separated."

As Nonno passed the customs station, a guard looked at his card and pulled him out of line. *"Perché?"* said Nonno (Why?). Without answering, the guard led him to a partitioned cage and slammed the door, locked. The guard resumed his position behind the customs desk. Nonno watched the same thing happen to Dom-

24

inic. He was also escorted to the same holding pen with Ottorino. Soon Mrs. Battaglia and the children arrived, and then the Maltese lady and the Arab and Frenchmen — all found themselves reunited. Then Nonno panicked. It couldn't be coincidence that these steerage passengers were together again. They began to look at each others' yellow tags to see what commonality isolated them. The Arab read "possible quarantine" checked off on each card. It had to have something to do with the dead man. Maybe they had been exposed to something communicable. Maybe they would be delayed—or worse, sent back. "My brother was going to meet me," cried Dominic in despair. "How will he know we are being held?"

Then Ottorino noticed another discrepancy. All the other yellow cards had been stamped "cleared" at the customs desk. His was not. He retraced the steps of his interrogation. He had given his name, Ottorino Bianchi. He had shown his passport and his wedding license to prove he was going to eventually send for his wife and son. The customs officer searched the manifest but could not find his name, and hence did not stamp his card. Then Ottorino remembered his wedding license read "Del Bianco," not Bianchi. The customs official must have been looking for Del Bianco after having examined the wedding license.

Nonno showed both documents to the Arab passenger, pleading with him in sign language to call the guard and explain the situation in English. The Arab understood Nonno's desperation and called an Italian interpreter to the grate of the pen.

"Please," intoned Nonno pitifully with the interpreter, "recheck the manifest. Everybody's card is marked 'cleared' and mine is not."

"You will have to go through customs again," said

the interpreter, and he unlocked the door, leading Nonno out and putting him at the end of the shortest baggage line. When he reached the desk the second time, there was a different official. Ottorino went through the same litany of questions and they inspected his belongings; this time they confiscated the can of sardines. He showed them his name was Bianchi and they found it on the manifest and his card was stamped "cleared."

He fully expected to be pulled out of line again to be returned to the isolation room, but the customs official didn't look at his card as the first one had done. The guard just said, "Keep moving." Ottorino wasn't about to object. He didn't have the nerve to look back at his still-distraught co-passengers who were sweating out "possible quarantine." He found himself back downstairs in a large room full of ticket agents and currency exchange booths.

They gave him fifty U.S. dollars for his *lire*. He expected more, but was afraid to protest because that could invite re-examination of his card that was still checked off with "possible quarantine." A ticket agent for one of the railroads did grab for his card, and it scared Nonno. The agent just wanted to see the final destination. When the agent saw San Francisco, he motioned Nonno to stand "over there." Nonno obeyed dutifully and soon found himself on another ferry headed west.

It was late at night. It had been a long, arduous day. Nonno was hungry and he wished he had his salami and cheese. But then his heart jumped for joy. An Italian family was embracing and crying and greeting their relatives on the dock. It was Dominic and the Battaglia family going crazy. Everyone must have been released, and the quarantine fear apparently had been overcome. And now, Ottorino was wondering what uncertainty lay before him.

✳ ✳ ✳

Nonno sat on his trunk in the ferry station and removed his yellow tag. He could read S.F. on it, but that was about all. He also removed the railroad confirmation he had purchased in France, and which he had been carrying under his shirt with the passport. He knew he had to take a train from somewhere, but when and how to get there—late at night, in a strange country, not knowing the language—was a formidable predicament. Then he got the idea of playing his guitar. It could attract authorities, or hopefully other Italians who would hear him sing and from whom he could seek help. Nothing happened through the first two songs. Then a passerby tossed him a coin, since he looked indigent. Nonno figured this person couldn't be an immigrant. Picking up the coin, he went after the stranger, offered to return the coin while holding up his train ticket and yellow tag. The passerby realized Nonno needed help. He examined the ticket and showed them to a waiting cab driver. There was a long discussion between the cab driver and the stranger. Finally, the latter pointed to a bus zone. On a nearby standard it read, Santa Fe. An empty yellow bus had Santa Fe printed on its side. A bus driver appeared from nowhere and motioned Nonno on board while pointing to the fare box. Nonno realized a fare was involved, but didn't understand how much. He took out Santina's five-dollar bill and held it up. Luckily the driver was honest and gave Nonno $4.50 in change. He was the only passenger, and a half-hour later the driver directed him to get off at a train station with a high ceiling and a big clock suspended over a dirty tile floor.

The suspended clock read 11:45. Nonno was wary, but mostly hungry. He hadn't eaten since early dawn before the anxieties of Ellis Island. He saw a clerk behind a wooden counter over which hung a sign that read "Hot dogs, 13¢." It appeared the attendant was cleaning up and ready to close shop. The clerk said something to Nonno, but Nonno shrugged to show it meant nothing to him. Then he held up one finger and pointed in the direction of some buns while reaching for the 50¢ change he had gotten from the bus driver. The clerk speared a soggy hot dog from barely warm water, placed it in the bun and pointed to the mustard and catsup, which Nonno ignored. The clerk gave him his change. Nonno removed the hot dog from the bun and bit into it first and then took a bite of the bun. He was so hungry it tasted good. Two more bites and seconds later he had inhaled the snack. The clerk stood in disbelief at the dispatch with which Nonno consumed his hot dog. Before he could recover from his surprise, Nonno was holding out the change and held up his finger once more. There were only two dogs left in the pot, and since the clerk was closing anyway, he placed both dogs side by side in a bun and, without asking Nonno, applied dabs of mustard and catsup along with some chopped onions he was ready to discard. The clerk only took a dime from the change Nonno was holding and mimicked biting into the meal so Nonno would not remove the hot dogs as he had done the first time. These were Nonno's first three hot dogs in America, and he ate them with gusto. This was a snack that was to sustain him many times in the railroad stations en route to California.

Nonno followed a black porter who befriended him and was handtrucking his trunk to a train that was to leave at 8:00 A.M. The porter put the trunk on a freight platform and then held out his hand for a tip. There was an awkward pause. Nonno didn't know how much to tip, but he sensed the porter was honest, as the latter had pointed out the track and train after studying Nonno's ticket information. Nonno held out the change from his hot dog purchases and the four one-dollar bills he had received from the bus driver.

"Hey, dagoman," said the porter, "Yo is gonna be ripped off. Don't nobody tell these immigrants 'bout money?" The porter took a dollar and closed Nonno's fist over the remaining cash and said, "Look, dagoman, a quarta wudda been fine, but yo all never had no quarta." Nonno stood there smiling and couldn't understand what the porter was saying, but he could mimic his speech. The two men returned to the station, which was mostly empty. Nothing much was happening at 1:30 in the morning except a man sweeping and a few ticket people who could be seen behind the bar-caged windows. Nonno was going to wait it out on one of the benches, but the porter said, "uh-uh, dagoman, yo'all cain't stay here. Cops ul getcha and yoal miss your train." Nonno surmised the porter liked talking out loud to himself, yet he was helpless to respond. Nonno tried to sit on the bench, but the porter was more emphatic.

"Cum wid me, dagoman"—and taking Nonno by the arm he led him to the porter station on the platform where, behind a door, the porters kept their carts and baggage tickets and related paraphernalia. The walls were covered with "girlie" calendars. Nonno raised his eyebrows to show approval. In a corner were several discarded swivel office chairs with torn upholstery. The porter pointed to two of them, and motioned Nonno to sit down and "rest yo feets." Nonno was sleeping before he ever hit the chairs.

"Wake up, dagoman, or yo is gonna miss yo train." Nonno was so grateful for what the porter had done for him that he reached into his pocket and offered the porter another dollar bill. "No need," said the porter. "Yo sho was tired." But he took the dollar. He personally led Nonno to a coach car. Behind it was a freight car, and the porter pointed to it saying, "Trunk in there." Nonno understood the word "trunk."

"Me, dagoman, say *grazie*—thank you."

The porter went up to a black conductor he seemed to know who was obviously going to work the train Nonno was about to board. "Take care of dis dagoman," said the porter. Then looking at Nonno, he said, "Yo got anuther dollar, don't cha?" Nonno pulled out the two remaining dollar bills from his pocket. The porter took one from Nonno and handed it to the conductor. "Dat's insurance," said the porter. "He's gonna take care of you." Nonno nodded, not really knowing what was going on, and soon he was smiling and waving goodbye to the porter from his coach seat.

It was a clear, sunny morning and Nonno heard the first of many "All aboard"s. The whistle blew and the engine lurched forward. The only thing that was bothersome was that the train was heading south, not west.

✳ ✳ ✳

How lucky, thought Nonno, there was nobody next to him or in front of his coach seat. He took his shoes off and reversed the seat in front of him so he could put his legs up and spread out his belongings and guitar.

He crumpled his coat into a headrest and stared eastward beneath the brim of his hat. The sun was before him; it arched over the train at noon, and soon its rays penetrated the window panes across the aisle. No doubt about it, he was traveling south, and this was confirmed when at dusk he spotted the constellation of Orion to the southwest. It was a little higher in the sky than he had known it in Italy. He began to worry he was on the wrong train. After every stop, the conductor to whom the porter had given Nonno's dollar came through the car calling for "tickets." He never even acknowledged Nonno's presence, and Nonno felt hurt. After all, the conductor had his dollar and Nonno hadn't realized any perceived benefit.

It had been several hours since the last stop and the relentless motion of the train heading south preyed more and more on Nonno's mind. He was distracted by the smell of food wafting from somewhere up ahead. Nonno remembered it had been a long time since his three hot dogs. He took his guitar and walked toward the engine, following the scent of food. When he came upon the dining car, he could see well-dressed passengers enjoying their evening meal.

As though it had been rehearsed, Nonno entered the dining car, positioned his hat at a rakish angle and began to sing "'Torna Soriento," with flair. The passengers believed this was a planned meal-time entertainment and welcomed Nonno's performance with applause and enthusiasm. The waiters didn't know what to make of the intrusion, but didn't protest. However, the conductor who had gotten the tip suddenly appeared and blocked Nonno's exit from the dining car. Nonno's sheepish smile did little to change the conductor's stare of disapproval. Nonno figured he was in trouble when the

31

conductor opened the dining car door and unceremoniously waved him out. Both men (and a silent guitar) stood between cars with the wind and rail noise that began to abate as the train was apparently coming to yet another stop. Nonno wondered if the train might be stopping because of his transgression. He was really worried when the conductor motioned to him to get off at a train station that looked like the rest he had seen most of the day.

While Nonno stood on the platform, the train backed on to a spur track. The conductor ignored Nonno as he waved a lantern and shouted with the engineer. No one else got on or off the train. As Nonno stood there, he heard the rattle of a horse-drawn wagon. A black woman was reining a tired horse; a young boy rode in the back. The boy was holding the handle to a wicker basket covered by a flour-sack towel. The boy's voice pierced through the darkness: "Paw, is dat you?"

"Yeah, Jason," said the conductor. It was the first time Nonno had seen the conductor smile. "Hey dagoman," said the conductor, "*vieni cui.*" The conductor had said "come here" in Italian. Then he pointed to the lady on the wagon. "*Moglie,*" he said (wife). Nonno was surprised the conductor knew some Italian words. Nonno pointed to the boy and asked, "*Figlio?*" (son). The conductor said, "*Si.*"

It made sense. The conductor must have picked up smatterings of languages serving immigrants through the New York station. It was obvious too, the conductor had somehow communicated to his family to be prepared to feed a fourth for dinner, because the conductor's wife began to spread four dinner portions on the tailgate of the wagon.

Nonno recognized a quarter of fried chicken for

each, sweet potatoes with honey, and some kind of corn porridge. There was also an iron pot of hot coffee. Nonno was moved by this display of hospitality and realized the conductor had taken his responsibility to "take care of dis dagoman" to heart. Nonno said, "*Grazie*," and he knew his thank-you was understood. Then the wife poured a small glass of berry wine and offered it to Nonno. "*Vino*," she said smiling, and indeed it was. A little too sweet for Nonno's taste, but the gesture of thoughtfulness made it taste like chianti.

The foursome ate their dinners bathed in weak moonlight and the window lights from the parked train. The wife began to hum something while she replaced dishes and utensils into the basket. Nonno quickly reached for his guitar and managed a few accompanying chords, but the lady stopped singing, slightly embarrassed.

"*Canta, canta*," (sing, sing) encouraged Nonno, and she began to hum again and then to vocalize, to the delight of her husband and son. Father and son clapped for the impromptu jam session that ended with a hiss from the train engine that shattered the harmony.

The conductor hastily pointed to the train and kissed his wife and child. He and Nonno reboarded the coach car. Forlorn hand waving disappeared in the darkness as the train re-entered the main track, which reminded Nonno he was still traveling south. But the memories of a pleasant repast and a full stomach of southern hospitality made Nonno speculate a dollar tip bought a lot in America.

❋ ❋ ❋

When Nonno awoke the next morning, the sun was behind his left shoulder and the train was now heading southwest. Nonno had to convince himself once and for all that he was on the right train. He sought out the conductor in the hope the latter's knowledge of some Italian could answer his nagging question.

"*Perché,*" (why) said Nonno to the conductor, "we no go west? We go *sud?*" In typical Italian fashion, Nonno was pointing and waving both hands to emphasize his question.

"We're taking the southern route," said the conductor—but he realized this hadn't answered the "why" of Nonno's question. The conductor said, "*Uno momento,*" then unlocked a utility cabinet at the entrance of the coach car and pulled out some old Santa Fe folders and advertising pieces that showed a map of the U.S. on the back with red-lined Santa Fe routes matrixed across the continent. The conductor penciled one of the red lines across the southern boundaries of the U.S., which showed Nonno they were headed for New Orleans. From there, he could follow the line through Texas, Arizona, New Mexico and Colorado with final stops in Los Angeles and north to Oakland, California.

Nonno was greatly relieved to see the map and motioned if he could keep it. To reinforce his skepticism he asked, "No Chicago?" Santina had written him she had gone through Chicago.

"No," said the conductor, "Santa Fe go southern route."

It seemed like a long way around to Nonno, but he accepted it and seemed content he was on the right train. He had heard about New Orleans and was now eagerly anticipating the destination. At each stop, Nonno read the name on the train stations and attempted to mark his progress on the map of his brochure. He soon realized the scale was unfamiliar and the distances were greater than he estimated. He recalled Santina's observation that America was indeed vast.

It was also apparent the train he was on spent more time on spur tracks and switching yards than on elapsed miles. And at this point, Nonno had no idea how long it might take to reach San Francisco.

That evening the conductor came through the coach car and specifically sought out Nonno. "*Vieni,*" he said, and then pointed to Nonno's guitar.

The two walked forward with the instrument to the dining car, which was closed; however, black cooks and waiters and one Caucasian railroad official were sitting around folding linens and reviewing the evening's menu. "This is the guitar player I told you about," said the conductor. As if on cue, the waiters and cooks began humming a spiritual and clapping their hands. The rhythm was foreign to Nonno, but not the key and modulations. After a few false starts, he was accompanying the syncopated melodies being sung. As Nonno learned to anticipate the tune, he embellished his chords with counterpoint and an occasional slap on the back of the guitar. This delighted the men; even the white boss laughed and clapped as he got into the spirit of the tunes. The rewarding surprise was that before the dining car opened, Nonno was presented with the evening fare of fried catfish, collard greens and coffee.

It wasn't the first time he had played for his supper, and it wouldn't be the last. He was grateful the conductor was still "taking care of him." However, the conductor let him know he was leaving the train *domani* (tomorrow).

Nonno got off at one of the stops and ran into the station to break a twenty-dollar bill. He asked for all ones and was accommodated. Then he found his conductor friend and gave him a dollar bill. Holding up another, he said, "Insurance?", recalling the New York porter's gesture that had won him the conductor's personal attention. "No insurance," said the conductor with a smile. "After tomorrow, you'll be on your own. It's been nice knowing you, dagoman. You'll be okay."

"Say *grazie* again to you *moglie* for nice dinner," said Nonno.

"I will," said the conductor.

Nonno sat, a bit dejected, on his coach seat the rest of the day. He was sorry he was losing a friend, and a little loneliness dampened his spirits. The next day the conductor came by to say his last goodbye. He was getting off somewhere in Louisiana a day before they were scheduled to reach New Orleans. The men shook hands and were never to see each other again.

In later years, Nonno became intolerant of bigoted remarks about black people. "They were the first Americans to be nice to me," he would say, "and they love music. I came to America by choice—they were brought here by force. They showed compassion for such as me, yet I found only a few who showed compassion for them."

Nonno's preconceived concept of the "land of the free" was compromised with regard to how blacks and American Indians were treated. He often related how this was his biggest ideological disappointment with America. He could understand prejudice against an immigrant as an intruder. He couldn't understand the prejudice against those who were born here.

5
Transitions

New Orleans was the biggest place he had seen since New York. The conductors made a point of instructing all passengers there would be a layover of eight hours. The train was scheduled to leave again by 7 P.M. Nonno was pleased he would have a day to enjoy and explore new surroundings. He set three priorities for himself. One, find a place to take a bath and wash his clothes; two, treat himself to a good, hot meal; three, write to Elisa and mail a letter to report he had survived his trip thus far.

He walked from the train station, checking his direction and the time on a clock in the station. He noticed the position and angle of the sun since he was clever in estimating the passage of time from mere observation. With his guitar slung on his back, he began looking for signs that might denote rooms and baths. He had seen many such signs at many of the other stops, but never had the time or courage to seek the accommodation.

There was a salt-water smell in the air. The train station, as it turned out, was pretty far from the city center. Nonno remembers seeing the "ocean" (actually the Mississippi Delta). He headed for the biggest cluster of buildings, which turned out to be commercial waterfront properties. Fishing fleets, shrimp trawlers and other maritime environments greeted Nonno as he relished the smell of cooked seafood.

He heard a fisherman speaking in French. Nonno's French, which he had picked up in his days of working in Le Havre, was good enough to allow him to ask directions for a room-and-bath house. Fifty cents later, he was being shown a second-story room in a pier building. The room contained a bed, an iron bathtub and a small bedtable and chair. A lady who had taken his money delivered a galvanized pan of hot water. She was "no lady," according to Nonno's description. She managed the rooms in this establishment, which Nonno figured must have done a brisk business at night.

But he was grateful for the privacy, and after soaking in the tub with an already used bar of scented soap, he soaked the clothes he was wearing. He draped his wrung-out garments about the room and wrapped himself with a blanket from the bed. At the small bedstand he began to write to Elisa on stationery he had taken from one of the train stations.

His heart poured out through the pen point. This was the first time he had the opportunity to relax and think about home, and it was therapeutic. His thoughts were forming so fast, he ran out of paper. He continued his letter on some crumpled drawer lining he found in the bedstand. When he got to the point of signing off with love, it was mid-afternoon and most of his clothes were dry.

Donning his wrinkled but clean clothes, he left and requested an envelope from the madam. She was polite and offered him several from an antique desk. "You coming back?" asked the madam.

"*Si,*" said Nonno, "I go eat—come back one hour, maybe two."

"That'll be another fifty cents after six o'clock," said the madam, "unless you spend the night with one of the girls." She pointed to a beautiful black girl who obviously had the mid-afternoon shift. Nonno smiled and waved his finger. "No girl—much hungry—food."

"You like fish?" asked the madam.

"*Si*," said Nonno.

"French restaurant two blocks down," said the madam, and she handed Nonno a business card from the desk. "Tell 'em Renée sent you."

Nonno folded his letter into one of the envelopes and proceeded in the direction of the restaurant. At the sight of cooked crayfish, large prawns, and mounds of clams, Nonno's mouth watered and a waiter walked up and said, "Bonjour, monsieur." At four in the afternoon, Nonno was the only customer in the restaurant. In French, the waiter explained they were nevertheless ready for customers. Nonno told the waiter where he was staying and flashed the card. The waiter gave a knowing wink, then asked, "How was it?" Nonno explained he had not gone there for the usual reason, but was due back on his train at 7:00 P.M.

The waiter did not press the explanation, nor did he believe it. But then Nonno asked him for a favor that lent credibility to his circumstances. He showed the waiter the letter to Elisa and asked if the waiter could mail it for him. Nonno explained he didn't know how the U.S. postal service worked, nor the cost. The waiter said, "Leave it to me"—and then began offering Nonno choices for his entrée. He chose steamed clams in a garlic sauce and an order of deep-fried prawns. With a fresh loaf of French bread, Nonno dug in. Then, to his surprise, the waiter brought out a bottle of French burgundy and Nonno recognized the label. It was a table wine of modest cost he had liked in France. The waiter joined him in the opposite chair, as there was no one else to serve, and Nonno related his experiences in France and why he had come to America.

At the end of the meal, Nonno pulled out two one-dollar bills—one for the waiter, one for his trouble to mail the letter. When he asked how much the dinner was, the waiter said, "One more dollar." The wine was compliments of the house where he was staying. It came out in the conversation that the madam owned the restaurant as well.

When Nonno got back to the room-and-bath house, there were several girls in the lobby in various stages of undress. He could hear activity upstairs. "How was the meal?" the madam asked. Nonno patted his stomach and made a circle with his thumb and forefinger, designating that the meal had been great. Then he went upstairs, relishing the fact that he still had about an hour before the train was to leave. But he hadn't counted on the effect of the hearty dinner and bottle of French wine. He fell asleep as he lay resting on the bed. The blast of a train whistle in the direction of the station woke him up. When Nonno saw the sun out his window barely touching the horizon, he knew he had missed his train.

✻ ✻ ✻

In retrospect, he was counting his blessings. He had a lot to be thankful for. He had survived the Atlantic, Ellis Island, a missed train in New Orleans that delayed him for weeks. He was grateful for the kitchen job in Renée's restaurant that allowed him to wait for the next train west; the station master who accepted his bribe and validated his train ticket so he could resume his journey; the 13¢ hot dogs when he couldn't play his guitar for meals; the fact that he had never gotten sick. And in Nonno's mind, the greatest miracle: he found his trunk waiting for him at the Oakland Mole. All these thoughts jumbled in no particular sequence clouded the reality that he was standing on the deck of the ferryboat *Eureka*, as it bumped into its slip at the Ferry Building in San Francisco. He had come farther west than Columbus; farther than he had ever thought possible— gratified to have reached the land's end of his hopes and of geography.

What with delays and mishaps, it was late March in 1906 and almost three months since he had kissed Elisa and Renato goodbye.

It was late afternoon and the Ferry Building lobbies were crowded with commuters and especially Santa Fe passengers like himself. Nonno piled his soiled drawstring sack and coat and guitar upon his trunk, and he approached a counter in the hope of inquiring about a city street map so he could proceed to Santina's address. Though unsuccessful, he spotted a promotional poster of San Francisco that identified the Ferry Building and lower Market Street. Nonno studied the poster for a long time and began to seek out names of major streets, but he could not find Vallejo, the address from which Santina and he had corresponded.

In frustration, he decided to gather his belongings, but to his dismay they were no longer where he had left them. His primary reaction was that he had become disoriented after studying the city poster; yet he was sure he had returned to the right spot. Then he blanched with pain at the possibility that his trunk and effects had been stolen. How far could someone get with a trunk and guitar? The perpetrator could not be far. Nonno ran to the exits looking right and left. He ran along the waiting cab lines. He retraced his steps to the deck from which he left the *Eureka*, trying to imagine where a thief would have gone when his back was turned as he read the poster. Anyone could have pretended to pick up his belongings as theirs, and Nonno was mad at himself for his carelessness. He had become conditioned to good luck and honesty across the country. The emotional impact of reaching San Francisco allowed him to let his defenses down, and now someone had taken advantage of that. In all innocence, he had permitted himself to become a victim.

He recalled everything he had packed. The gift for Santina, letters for her from her friends that he had been instructed to deliver. But nothing hurt more than the loss of his guitar. It had been his solace, his meal ticket, his traveling companion, his link to the values he held most dear. Now it was gone — as if part of his body had been wrenched from him.

Nonno wanted to cry, but his pride forbade it. A disillusioned immigrant wandered aimlessly about the San Francisco Ferry Building at the point of despair.

How could he face his sister in the wake of this carelessness? He could not allow himself to crawl upon her doorstep as a destitute charity case. His funds were close to depleted; only about twenty dollars were left in cash in his passport, which he still wore under his shirt. Thank God for that discipline, or he might have lost his money too.

As a last act of faith he sought and approached a uniformed policeman at Embarcadero and Market streets. The policeman was preoccupied giving directions to another immigrant family. Nonno heard some of the individuals of the family speaking to each other in Italian. Without waiting to talk to the policeman, Nonno voiced his desperation: "I've been robbed; do you think this officer can help me?"

The empathy from the members of the Italian family deluged Nonno with questions. "When? How? When did it happen?" The apparent head of the family broke off his conversation with the policeman. "My name is Pioli," he said. "What's the matter?"

"My name is Bianchi; I've just been robbed of everything I owned."

"Where are you from?" asked Pioli. Among Italians, this query is the first and most important question— more important than who you are, because where you are from reinforces preconceived prejudices.

"Pisa," said Nonno, thinking that even among Toscani, few would know about Bientina.

"We are from Lucca," said Pioli. "Not far." Pioli seemed to have better command of broken English than Nonno. He pleaded Nonno's case to the policeman, but the latter shook his head.

"It's no use," said the cop. "Your stuff is gone. There are professionals here who prey on new arrivals. Some are so brazen they pretend to help immigrants with their luggage and walk away knowing they can never be identified. Tell your friend his stuff is gone."

Pioli didn't have to translate. Nonno saw the look of helplessness on both the faces of the policeman and Mr. Pioli.

The latter's feelings for Nonno's plight prompted an attempt at optimism. "Cheer up, Bianchi," said Pioli, "you can join my family. We're on our way to my brother who lives in Marin County. We were farming in the Delta area for about six months, and my brother wrote

to me about work in Marin. They are building a funicular to the top of Mt. Tamalpais. I am sure there will
be work there for you too."

"I cannot impose," said Nonno. "Besides, my sister
is waiting for me."

"What's a few more weeks?" said Pioli. "You can
earn a few dollars, get yourself on your feet and then
join your sister." Somehow the logic of Pioli's suggestion had appeal. It at least postponed Nonno's dilemma
of facing his sister penniless and embarrassed.

Nonno followed Pioli and his wife and young daughter and another gentleman who later was introduced by
Pioli as his cousin from Stockton. They entered the Ferry
Building again and boarded another steamboat destined
for Sausalito. "I'll repay you," said Nonno humbly, but
his voice lacked conviction; he was still smarting as if
he had been a beaten puppy dog. The last few hours had
been a bad dream, and the nightmare replayed itself over
and over in Nonno's mind. It was as if he had lost the
lead in the last few yards of a marathon race.

※ ※ ※

Pioli's brother had to be his twin, thought Nonno.
They looked so much alike there could be no doubt they
were related. The entourage greeted each other and introduced Nonno as newly arrived from Italy, and he was
made to feel welcome. They walked from the Sausalito
dock to a flatbed truck with wooden spokes and hard rubber tires. Pioli's brother hauled produce with this vehicle from his small farm near San Rafael, which was where
they were headed.

Nonno could not see much from the back of the
truck since it was around nine o'clock at night—but Pioli

pointed out the silhouette of Mt. Tam and told Nonno that that was where they would be reporting for work the next day.

At the Pioli farm Nonno was housed in a barn loft and was told to try on some bib overalls and rubber knee-high boots used by the truck-farming help. This would be appropriate attire for the work on Mt. Tam.

The plan was for Pioli's brother to drive his newly arrived brother and Nonno to the labor camp at Mt. Tam early next morning. Hundreds of laborers were required for a proposed funicular to the top of the mountain. Pioli's brother had learned his neighbor's son was a foreman on the job for the general contractor and this connection is what had lured the Piolis from Stockton to Marin.

The work campsite at the base of Mt. Tam was a mass of humanity, and in the early morning light all Nonno could see were Chinese laborers—thousands of them. Pioli found the foreman at a pre-arranged tent complex and introduced his brother and Nonno as his friends.

The foreman, a young and rugged fellow, greeted Bianchi and Pioli. "You're going to be *barella* men," he said, and the men nodded as if they knew what that meant.

Nonno whispered to Pioli, "What's a *barella?*"

"I don't know," said Pioli.

They both thanked Pioli's brother for the ride, and Nonno made a point of thanking him for his work clothes, and then the wooden-wheeled truck disappeared into the overcast to the east.

"You two *barella* men, come with me," said the foreman. The three men passed a lot of Chinese coolies dressed in Chinese conical straw hats. They were shoveling a trail along the inclined slope with picks and hand shovels. Dirt was being carried in baskets on bamboo sling poles and dumped on the downhill slope of the cut. Farther up the mountain, as the grade became steeper, men carrying *barellas* rotated between the diggers and where the earth was needed to fill depressions as the work progressed.

A *barella* was a two-man pallet or stretcher that carried earth. Two 8- to 10-foot eucalyptus saplings were placed parallel, and across them light planks were nailed, making a square about four by four feet. Two men carried this arrangement like a sedan chair loaded with earth from the diggers and then the load was carried and dumped with great precision in the depressed areas of the downhill slope where the engineers supervised the compaction of the earth that later would become the base on which the funicular track was to be laid.

The steep inclination of the slopes made wheelbarrows impractical for a single man trying to balance a load on a tire and fighting gravity — and besides, it was too slow.

Nonno and Pioli became pretty compatible and learned the best gait and rhythm that permitted them to load and dump. They were paid by the trip, or load, which was defined as that amount of earth that stayed on the *barella* until it spilled off the edges. Two strong men could carry about 200 pounds with good agility unless they hit rocky soil, which was harder to carry. The hazards were the tripping or falling of either partner, which obviously spilled the load. This required the team of men to re-shovel the *barella*, which lost time and money. Competition soon developed among the *barella* teams. Pioli and Nonno were not among the best, but as they gained experience, they mastered the art of "not spilling," and they learned from the Chinese pole carriers the bouncing gait that helped them carry pallets of dirt with less fatigue. The empty back-trips were rest times when one could set one's own pace. The *barella* jobs were sought after for this reason, as opposed to the Chinese diggers who toiled constantly with few breaks. The Chinese, generally of smaller stature, were great at carrying baskets of earth, but the volume was small. *Barella* men were generally the heavy "jocks" and they developed their upper bodies and arms in short order.

Nonno and Pioli suffered the first three days. Living conditions were not the best. Open showers, mess-hall lines for food service, and tent accommodations for sleeping were crude and makeshift. The rainy terrain and red-stained earth of Marin raised havoc on clothes and general hygiene.

On the plus side, the food wasn't bad. Eggs and hot cereal in the morning; pigs' feet for lunch; stews and vegetables and soups for dinner . . . and a lot of hot dogs and hamburger steak. The Chinese workers had their own meals of fish and rice brought in daily on the steamboats from San Francisco. At times, Nonno wished he could eat their meals.

Except for those who gambled, there was nowhere to spend one's pay. The Chinese were paid in silver coin; the Caucasians were paid in gold dust or gold coin, if they chose reimbursement weekly. Nonno chose the latter, for on weekends he could return to the Pioli ranch to safeguard his cash. This income became the beginnings of the savings Nonno would send to Elisa for her eventual fare to America.

As the weeks went by, both Nonno and the Pioli family were grateful for their jobs. Nonno and Pioli contributed to the ranch and household for their weekend stays on the farm and the convenience of a change of clothes and laundering needs. The Pioli women also packed lunches that lasted the men through the early days of the week. Cold cuts, fried rabbit, salami, risotto and fresh fruit complemented the camp menus on the job.

As the ground breaking approached the summit, *barella* teams found harder footing. Pioli was instrumental in convincing the foreman he and Nonno could do better unloading cross ties for the rails that were being placed at the lower elevations. The cross ties came by train from the logging camps up north. This was great duty for Nonno and Pioli because during the slack periods between trains, they could rest and enjoy their home-cooked fare.

News and supplies from San Francisco were as frequent as the ferry boat schedules, and one day both Pioli and Nonno were excited to hear that Enrico Caruso was coming to San Francisco to sing. Nonno had never heard Caruso sing in person in Italy, and here was a musical oportunity he could not resist. Pioli was a music lover too, and the pair began talking about plans to attend the San Francisco concert. Nonno also felt it was time to try to find his sister Santina. He had forgotten the theft of his belongings, though not his guitar, which he missed. His accumulation of earnings had permitted a new wardrobe and he felt he was now presentable. It was time to graciously bow out from the hospitality of the Piolis, to whom he had become so indebted. Pioli's prophecy had been correct and Nonno was back on his feet. It was time to seek out Santina while "employed" and not become a liability to whatever economic circumstances she might be in.

The latrine facilities at Mt. Tam were primitive slit trenches for the hundreds of workers. Nonno was answering the call of nature on the morning of April 6th prior to reporting for breakfast. Suddenly, nature began "calling back," as he put it. A rumble and subsequent tremor throughout the countryside turned the camp into frenzy and chaos. This was the morning of the 1906 earthquake in San Francisco.

From atop Mt. Tam, Nonno could see the columns of smoke forming, harbingers of the fires that ultimately destroyed most of San Francisco. Early ferry boats brought news of the devastation and exaggerated reports of death and destruction. Work was suspended as workers clamored to the Sausalito docks trying to get to San Francisco to learn about loved ones. Refugees brought back tales of the damage and martial law. Nonno feared for Santina; he felt guilty because he had detoured to Marin before seeing her. He told Pioli he had to leave camp and was determined to find Santina.

6

Search for Santina

At the Sausalito ferry slip there was utter confusion. Refugees were coming from San Francisco to avoid the fire, reported to be out of control. Only personnel linked to the emergency relief were allowed to cross the bay back to San Francisco. Nonno saw some firemen struggling with a pumper wagon as they tried to roll the equipment onto the auto deck of the ferry. In his bib overalls and rubber boots, he looked like a fireman, so he rushed and put his shoulder to the wheel and got on board the ferry without suspicion. He hid in the men's room until he knew the ferry was under way. At the San Francisco dock, he repeated his assistance by pushing off the fire equipment. Then he strolled away casually, hoping to find Vallejo Street, where Santina lived.

The ferry docked at what is now Aquatic Park. From there, Nonno was able to walk south on Van Ness, but noticed that guards prevented entry at every eastbound intersection. Following directions prepared by Pioli, he came to Vallejo Street. Santina's address was east of Van Ness in the roped-off area earmarked for backfire and dynamiting to cope with the fire started by the quake. Nonno concluded just by the activity that the likelihood that Santina would be at home was remote. But he could at least leave a note to tell her he had arrived.

He approached a soldier guarding the Vallejo intersection. Nonno pointed east and showed the soldier Santina's address—"*Mi* sister," he said. The soldier waved him off and Nonno proceeded south on Van Ness to

Pacific. At that intersection, there seemed to be more activity. He took advantage of everyone's preoccupation and started to stroll eastward, and he made it to Polk Street unchallenged. He backtracked to Vallejo and eastward up the hill, looking for Santina's address on the fronts of the houses. It was a three-story flat noticeably empty and probably evacuated the day before. Nonno scribbled a note to Santina and slipped it under the door sill. As he did so he heard a shot and the shatter of glass from the transom over his head. He whirled around to find three solders pointing their rifles at his head. "You're under arrest," said the one who fired the shot–his weapon was still smoking. Martial law had been invoked to prevent looting, and anybody in an unauthorized area was fair game. It was a "shoot first, ask questions later" situation. Nonno tried to reach for his passport and to explain why he was there, but he wasn't given the chance. The military men handcuffed him and he was soon being led at gunpoint toward Van Ness Avenue.

A military command post had been set up at the corner of Broadway and Van Ness, and Nonno was taken there handcuffed. As he pondered his fate, a team of horses pulling an open wagon rattled up. It stopped at the military tent and two men began unloading picks and shovels and cases of explosives that had come from the Presidio. Nonno heard the drivers talking in Italian.

"*Scuza*" (excuse me), said Nonno, "can you help me? I've been arrested trying to find my sister. I've done nothing wrong. My name is Bianchi."

"My name is Moro," said the driver, "and this is my partner, Gemingnani. They confiscated our team and wagon to help out in the earthquake emergency. We've been hauling stuff for the army all day."

"When did you get here?" asked Gemingnani.

"About a month ago," replied Nonno. "I've been working on the Mt. Tam funicular. I came today to find my sister Santina, who lives on Vallejo."

"You weren't supposed to be there," said Moro.

"I found that out," said Nonno. "They shot at me."

"You were lucky," said Moro. "They could have killed you on the spot."

"I've seen it happen," chimed in Gemingnani.

"Where are you from?" came the inevitable question. "You speak Toscano."

"Bientina," said Nonno.

"Huh, a Bientinese," said Moro knowingly. "We're from Lucca, been here about a year."

"Hey, *Capitano*," said Moro to the apparent commander in charge. "This man is my *paisano*—he's not a looter. We're from the same part of Italy." Moro Campi and Julio Gemingnani had built up a bit of credibility for their cooperation the past few days in helping the military haul supplies on their teamster wagon.

The "Capitano" (could have been a sergeant) wasn't too eager to address the paper work associated with the arrest. "If you sign for him," said the *Capitano*, "we'll let him go."

"I sign," said Moro. "This is a good man." He winked at Nonno to give him assurance the situation would be resolved. The arresting guard removed Nonno's cuffs and Nonno immediately clasped his hands around Moro's in gratitude.

"*Grazie mille*," said Nonno, "I apologize if I have imposed."

"No bother, Bianchi," said Moro. "Stay out of trouble, and I hope you find your sister."

The men parted, never to see each other again. But there was a quirk of fate in this encounter. When Nonno was relating this part of his story to me, my mother over-heard his narrative of the conversations with the team-sters. "My God," said my mother, "That was my father and my uncle!" Two future fathers-in-law had met, never to know their respective children would someday marry each other! At this point in time, my dad was a little boy in Italy, and my mom had just been born in San Francisco.

✳ ✳ ✳

Nonno hadn't the vaguest idea what to do next, other than contemplate returning to Marin County. As he started to leave, the soldier who had fired the shot and arrested him yelled, "Hey you, come here!" The soldier was leading a detail of military men and some civilians at gunpoint to a job to clear debris from the havoc of the earthquake. Nonno realized explaining his "exoneration" from arrest would be futile. He reluctantly obeyed the command, and soon found himself clearing, hauling, and loading rocks and rubble to clear the streets for rescue and fire teams. Many times during the day's frustrations he entertained notions to "bug off," but he was thwarted by the rifle of the guard, whose trigger finger insured that the conscripted helpers kept work-ing. Nonno wasn't about to tempt fate nor the soldier's license to shoot under the circumstances of martial law.

The hot and dirty tasks lasted until sunset and Nonno's clothes, along with those of the other work-ers, became tattered, torn, soiled, and permeated with ash and dust from the day's work. The detail was marched to the Presidio that evening and they were led to a Red Cross tent where civilian workers were handing out bundles of clothes to earthquake victims who had had to abandon their homes.

One of the men on detail with Nonno protested that their clothes had been ruined and that they should be recompensed. The complaint permitted the group to claim some clothing from the Red Cross. But Nonno never expected what he found in his wrapped handout.

The description of his feelings as he unwrapped his new clothes became a classic story repeated in my younger days whenever the subject of the San Francisco earthquake came up. The bundle contained a magician's tuxedo from some theatrical troop—complete with wide satin stripes on the pants, pop-up top hat, and feather flower bouquets hidden in the sleeves.

Nonno's sense of humor encouraged him to don his new outfit, to the delight of his fellow workers and the hysterical laughter and applause of others around him. The ridiculous outfit, complete with tails, was in stark contrast to the tensions and stresses of the day. It was comic relief timed perfectly under the circumstances, and Nonno was ham enough to pull it off. Looking every bit like the character Emperor Norton, Nonno popped up his top hat, waved his feathered bouquets, and to the applause of his intimate crowd, he disappeared with a low bow into a wooded section of the Presidio. He thus "escaped" his work detail. He soon discovered that walking around in a tuxedo in the wake of a disaster allowed him a lot of latitude in behavior. Frankly, he recalls, people avoided him like the plague.

Nonno returned once more to Vallejo Street in the hope of finding out something about Santina. Many people were attempting to return to their homes at dusk. In the meantime, martial law had eased up. Santina was nowhere to be found, but Nonno saw a lady in the lower flat of the dwelling. He hesitated about his appearance in the ill-fitting magician's tux. After removing his top hat and coat to look more conventional, he knocked on the door and showed Santina's picture, which he still carried in his passport. "*Mi* sister," he pointed, "she live here?"

"Yes, I knew Santina," said the lady. Nonno's hopes were stirred at the lady's admission to recognizing the picture. "She left about a month ago with her husband, Pellegrini."

"*Si, si,*" said Nonno, a bit excited. He reacted to hearing the name Pellegrini.

"They went north to Eureka," said the lady.

"Eureka?" said Nonno.

"Yes," repeated the lady. "I'm the manager here. They paid their last month's rent and went to Eureka."

"Where Eureka?" asked Nonno.

"Up north," said the lady.

"Me go," said Nonno, and the conversation ended.

Nonno was relieved to conclude that Santina and her husband had to have missed the earthquake, but how would he find her in Eureka? He hadn't the slightest notion where Eureka was, nor how to get there.

Nonno walked to the Muni pier, where he observed passengers being allowed to board the ferries without paying a fare. Evacuation was still being encouraged, and Nonno was allowed to board amid stares one would expect for an eccentric in a top hat and tux. Since Nonno couldn't hide from his attire, he periodically reinforced his image for his own amusement by swinging his arm, allowing the weighted feather bouquet to slide down his sleeve and into his hand, which he then flipped for all to view, as if by "magic." This self-taught trick got better with each try, and invariably brought embarrassed smiles from those in his vicinity.

It was a long walk from the Sausalito ferry dock to San Rafael and the Pioli ranch. Nonno knew his chances of getting a ride were slim, especially in his ridiculous magician's outfit. Luckily, he was also on the main route to the Mt. Tam work area. A supply truck driver recognized him and saved him many miles toward the Pioli homestead. It was late evening when Nonno arrived at the ranch, and after demonstrating his feathered flower trick, he kept the Pioli family in stitches relating the story of his arrest and how he was conscripted to work at gunpoint. Though disappointed about not finding Santina, he was happy to learn she was headed for Eureka, wherever that was.

"It's pretty far north," said Pioli. "You can get there by ferry up the coast, or you can catch a logging train on its return haul. Since there are many logging camps, you could even work your way up."

The cost of the ferry trip was out of the question, for it would deplete the little money Nonno had managed to save. But the prospects of following the train tracks north didn't seem impossible. There was much discussion about Nonno writing to Elisa in the hope Santina had corresponded in the meantime and given her new address. But everybody agreed that a response would take a long time, and the idea was dropped. Nonno felt he had imposed on the Piolis long enough. It was time to move on.

Equipped with a donated pair of knee-high boots, a blanket and knapsack, Nonno bid adieu to the Piolis — thanking them for rescuing him in his time of need. Blinded by his resolve and determination to find Santina, he proceeded to "walk" to Eureka, a distance of over

350 miles from the Bay Area. Nonno had no indication of how long this "walk" would take, nor the obstacles that he was to confront en route.

By the end of the first day, he had reached the out-skirts of Novato and was frustrated walking the railroad ties of a track that led him north. The length of his stride was too long to step on the railroad ties one at a time, and too short to attempt two ties per stride. He finally resolved to negotiate the gravel bed beside the tracks, but the slope of the track bed invariably edged him toward brambles and bushes and weeds that made walking difficult. It rained the first night of his trek, and his only blanket proved useless against the elements. He almost decided to turn back, but the "shine" on the rails told him the track was obviously being used. Surely a train would be coming along soon. The next day one did, and Nonno had no difficulty hopping onto a flat-bed car. The train was traveling north, and that was all he cared about.

＊ ＊ ＊

By evening his clothes had dried and the blanket allowed Nonno a good night's sleep on the flat car. A swerve in the track jostled him awake the next morn-ing and the sun was already pretty high. The clear skies and sunshine warmed his bones, and the beauty of the redwood forest impressed Nonno as he reached into his sack for some stale bread and cheese that had been provided by the Piolis. Because he was riding between two box cars, Nonno couldn't be seen from the engine unless the train was rounding a sharp curve. On these instances, he lay still under his blanket to hide. The en-gineers probably were used to riders on the freight train and could not have cared less. But Nonno wasn't taking any chances of running afoul of the law or the railroad employees. At the first stop, he darted into the forest cover some 50 yards from the tracks. From this cover, he could watch the switching or loading of cars and look for his opportunity to jump back on board. At a place called Ukiah, the engine shut down completely; the silence told him his ride was over, at least for the present. He moved on to the train platform as if he belonged there, and once again wondered where the winds of fate would take him.

On a spur track traveling south, Nonno saw a lumberjack pumping a teeter-totter hand car. He flagged him down, and surprisingly the lumberjack stopped.

"What can I do for you?" asked the lumberjack.

Nonno's keen ear caught a hint of French accent. "*Parlez-vous Français?*" asked Nonno.

"*Oui,*" responded the French Canadian.

In Italianized French, Nonno explained that he was looking for work and hoping to get to Eureka.

"I can use your arms," said the Frenchman, pointing to the teeter handle of the rail cart.

Soon both men were making good time into a wilderness of redwoods; and after about three or four miles, they pulled into a lumber campsite reeking of acrid smoke. Lumberjacks were chaining charred redwood logs onto trucks and trailers. The smallest log Nonno saw was in excess of six feet in diameter and twenty feet long, and even bigger ones were stacked pyramid style.

The smell of the pungent, damp smoke was everywhere, and it quickly penetrated one's clothes. Eyes watered, for in addition to the smell of charred logs destined for milling, the camp smoldered in columns of smoke hanging in the air.

"Was there a forest fire?" asked Nonno in all innocence.

"Of course," said the Frenchman, in a matter-of-fact
voice. "That's how we clear the brush to get to the bigger trees. In fact, if you work here, that's what you'll
be doing." He pointed to a cylindrical tank that could
be strapped on one's back. "You'll be wearing that," said
the Frenchman, and he went on to explain to Nonno
how men referred to as "backfires" went about controlled
burning of a sector of forest so that the loggers could
go in later to cut the trees that withstood the pillage.

Nonno learned to flare or concentrate his flame-
thrower as he teamed up with other "backfires." Though
the work and pay was the best he had experienced, he
could not get used to the slaughter of forest animals that
ran out of the inferno charred and burning in pain and
panic to their inevitable death.

"Why must we burn?" asked Nonno. "It kills the
smallest trees, and working in smoke seems ridiculous."
His questions were never answered. One morning the
Frenchman told him he had better move on. Nonno
didn't mind losing this job. The waste and carnage didn't
justify the economics.

He felt good walking north again away from that
ugly camp. The sight of deer, birds and chipmunks
raised his spirits until he came upon the railroad tracks
again. Then the prospect of striding the ties one or two
at a time reminded him how uncomfortable it was to
walk the rails.

7

Forest Interludes

Sleeping under a railroad culvert had not been pleasant. Nonno gathered his stuff at first light and shortly came upon a dirt road crossing east to west. He headed west in hopes of finding some sort of civilization. He was hungry.

The road soon crossed another that was paved and ran parallel to the train tracks. He would travel north again on easier footing and with the outside chance of hailing some kind of vehicle. After two hours of walking, the trees on each side of the road just got taller and bigger. Thick ferns and underbrush and an occasional sign of wildlife seemed to protest Nonno's presence. Deer and squirrels ruffled the stillness, and the road got dark as the peaks of the trees blocked out the sun.

The receptivity of one's senses increases when one is alone. The senses of smell and hearing strain. It was faint at first. Smoke, maybe cooking smoke. Nonno's empty stomach gurgled, and it interfered with his attempt to determine the direction of the smell. Around the next bend he spied a mailbox at the head of a foot trail headed west. Wishful thinking persuaded him the smoke smell was coming from the direction of the path.

He opened the mailbox, not knowing what he might do with anything in it. It was empty. Cautiously, he proceeded down the trail, pushing away ferns at shoulder height. Now the smoke smell took on the fragrance of baked bread, and he almost broke into a jog. It had to be food. But soon a dog's bark warned of his presence, and he emerged into a clearing in front of a thatch-roofed log cabin. The telltale smoke he had detected miles back hung close to the ground, and the smell of baking made him all the more ravenous.

He kept an eye on the barking dog as he approached the cabin door, sensing he had to have been seen by any occupant.

"Stay where you are," said a voice, as the cabin door opened slowly, and, though Nonno hadn't understood the words, the business end of a double-barreled shotgun needed no translation.

Nonno froze and slowly lifted his hands to communicate his submissive intentions. But his hands dropped in surprise when the speaker came into view.

She was beautiful! Long, light brown, braided hair and penetrating green eyes, about mid-twenties, thought Nonno, erect posture and milk-white skin. Even though she was wearing bib overalls and logger's knee boots, Nonno could not help admiring an ample bosom behind the gun sight.

The silence seemed interminable. Then Nonno motioned to his mouth and said, *"Fáme,* hungry, please, food?"

Satisfied she had the upper hand and the shotgun, the woman called off her dog, and the barking was reduced to a guttural growl.

"Wait there," she said, and the gun barrel dropped. The woman retreated into the cabin, leaving the door open so she could see both Nonno and her dog.

Nonno didn't dare move under the penetrating glare of the seated mongrel, whom he suspected could tear him apart at the right command from its mistress.

Nonno watched the woman scoop some butter into a skillet on a cast-iron wood stove. Soon she brought out some hot, buttered biscuits. She smiled at Nonno as she put down the pan; however, she still cradled the shotgun in the other arm.

"*Grazie,*" said Nonno, and he inhaled about nine biscuits, to the astonishment of both the woman and her dog.

"You must be starving," she said, as she returned inside the cabin to mix another batch. This time she brought them out without her shotgun, though it was leaning on the door jamb within easy reach. Nonno had managed to pet the dog in the interim, allowing the latter free license to sniff him out. It appeared the anxieties were over and a little trust and humanity prevailed.

"What's your name? What are you doing here?"

"Name, Bianchi," said Nonno, and he reached for his passport. "Me *Italiano,* go find sister—Eureka."

"Eureka!" echoed the woman. "That's way up north."

"*Norte, si,*" said Nonno with a smile, and pointing north. "Eureka. Me go now; thank you for food. *Molto buono.*"

"Wait." She went back into the cabin and came out with some fruit. "You take," she said. Realizing the language difficulties, she put an orange and a pear into his pocket.

"No," said Nonno, "I no can pay—you keep."

"You can work."

"Work?" questioned Nonno. She pointed to a pile of stumps that obviously had been waiting to be split for firewood. "You cut wood, I'll give you food for your trip to Eureka." Nonno only understood Eureka, but he figured out the woman wanted help and he needed provisions.

"Okay," smiled Nonno. "Me work." Nonno's skill with a double-bladed ax became very apparent. By midday, he had split every stump in sight, and splintered kindling was strewn about the yard and clearing. The dog delighted in chasing chips; the woman smiled at Nonno through the cabin window, and once brought him a glass of cold tea.

It was late afternoon as he washed by a half barrel being fed cold, clear water from a pipe. He buttoned his shirt in preparation to leave, half hoping he might be invited for another meal.

His hostess came out of the cabin and extended her hand. "*Grazie,*" she said in Italian. "Thank you for all that you have done. Must you leave?"

"*Che?*" said Nonno.

"Can you stay? I can't let you go at night." Nonno wasn't sure about the invitation, nor what it implied.

He pointed to her wedding ring. "Your husband come?"

"No," she answered, "my husband is working in lumbercamp. He's a lumber mill foreman."

"What you name?" asked Nonno. He realized he had not asked before, and now, on the verge of accepting more hospitality, somehow it seemed important.

"Ann," came the reply. "Ann McCloud. You can stay. I have an extra bunk. Come." She motioned Nonno into the cabin that betrayed its rustic exterior.

The kitchen area he had seen from the door took up about a third of the floor space. The floor was planked and extended to a cozy stone fireplace. Steps of the same stone led up to an attic area, obviously bedroom space. A partitioned wall at ground level had several doors leading to pantry, storage, and bathroom. Spartan, thought Nonno, but comfortable and clean.

His glance caught two significant things that captivated his attention. The kitchen table had been preset for two. It was clear Ann had anticipated Nonno would stay. On the mantle of the fireplace there was a guitar with the E-string missing. He didn't know how to be a gracious guest and curb his urge to pick up the instrument without permission. To break his self-conscious staring, he said, "You play?"

"No," responded Ann, "It belongs to my husband, but there's a string missing."

Nonno picked up the guitar and retuned the remaining strings, ignoring the missing strand. He then began strumming chord modulations and doing staccato finger work that took Ann by surprise.

It felt so good to be playing a guitar once again, and in a sotto voce, he delved into one *stornello* after another until Ann stopped her meal preparation and literally applauded with enthusiasm.

"You're terrific," she exclaimed.

Nonno didn't know what terrific meant, and ignoring the praise, he asked, "You sing?"

"Sometimes," Ann replied, a bit sheepishly.

"*Canta, canta*," Nonno insisted, and soon humming and improvised lyrics and false starts permeated the cozy cabin with accompaniment that embellished Ann's voice, which Nonno recognized as that of a promising contralto.

"Food's ready," interrupted Ann. She removed a roasting chicken with potatoes and onions from the cast-iron stove. On top of the stove was a flat pan with a variation of the biscuits Nonno had tasted that morning. The two sat at opposite ends of a crude slab redwood table under the light of a kerosene lamp and the flame of the fireplace.

Nonno made short work of his pieces of chicken. The potatoes were scrumptious, and through it all Ann smiled, visibly pleased to have her culinary skill devoured by so appreciative an appetite. Coffee and a mason jar of home-preserved peach halves comprised the dessert.

Nonno felt the obligation to help clean the table, and Ann was noticeably touched by this consideration. She began telling Nonno how inconsiderate her husband was in such matters. Nonno could only understand a minimum of what she was saying, but he detected regret and sadness in Ann's tone of voice.

The casual brushing of their bodies as they replaced pots and pans from the sink to proper pantries communicated the desire of one and the frustrations of the other. Nonno felt he had better fight the urge by picking up the guitar again with the pretense of re-tuning it because of the missing string.

They both sat in front of the fireplace, and Nonno wondered if he was in Ann's husband's chair. What if her husband suddenly came in? Would he understand his wife's kindness to a stranger? The potential for intimacy was too threatening for Nonno. He finally asked, "Where I sleep?" Ann pointed to one of the doors leading to a rear service porch. Against the wall was a wooden framed cot strung with interlaced hemp rope. On top of that was a down-filled mattress. Clean linens had been meticulously folded, and a pillow and extra blankets graced the far end.

Nonno sat on the bed and smiled, anticipating a comfortable night's rest. Then Ann adjusted a window to allow a minimal amount of cold air, and fussed as if encouraging a small child to bed. She stepped forward and kissed Nonno's forehead, bidding him goodnight as she closed the door. Nonno wondered if his blush was visible in the twilight of the room as Ann left and went upstairs to her bedroom directly above the space where

Nonno was bedded down. Nonno washed at the basin, removed his clothes and relished the clean sheets and privacy. But he fought off sleep listening to Ann audibly preparing for bed above his ceiling. He wondered how any husband could abandon such a lovely woman to the solitude of a forest. It didn't make sense, but then he thought, "I've done no less to Elisa and Renato." This was a sad world, he mused in the drowsiness of his comfort. He basked in the memory of how great it felt to strum a guitar again, and coupled with the thoughts of his pleasant meal, he ruffled up his pillow and fell into a deep sleep.

※ ※ ※

There was no mistaking the smell of frying bacon the next morning. Ann was jostling stove lids, probably in an attempt to wake her overnight guest. Nonno climbed into his clothes and emerged, a bit bleary-eyed. He noticed Ann was still in her bib overalls, but her hair was braided into a pug at the back of her neck.

"How do you like your eggs?" she smiled. Nonno didn't understand. Ann held up two eggs. Nonno nodded approval, but could not answer her question. She broke the eggs in a skillet in which the bacon had been frying, then motioned with a fork in the air to communicate if Nonno wanted them scrambled. Nonno motioned no, and moved the pan to a cooler corner of the stove to let the eggs simmer sunny-side up. After his comfortable sleep and fine breakfast (the first in a long time), Nonno was anxious to leave, but he could see that Ann was troubled. He thought she was gathering her thoughts on how to communicate something to Nonno. Finally it came out. "You stay one more day?" Ann said in a deliberate, almost hopeful, way. Nonno understood and relished the opportunity for more of the wonderful hospitality, but at the same time he knew the longer the stay, the harder the parting. He was determined to resume his journey to Eureka.

"All wood chopped," said Nonno, implying he had earned his keep. He was wondering about the possible arrival of Ann's husband—an awkward encounter if it happened, and one he'd rather avoid.

"No chop wood," said Ann. "Help me fix cooler— then you can leave tomorrow—*domani!*" Her attempt at Italian was in the hope of lending credibility to her request. Nonno had no idea what a "cooler" was, nor what Ann hoped to achieve by what he perceived to be a delaying tactic.

Nonno ate his bacon and eggs in silence, and Ann must have assumed this silence meant consent, for without further conversation she led Nonno outside along a babbling brook that he later learned was the main water supply to the cabin. About fifty yards upstream the two came upon a curious structure astride the brook. Redwood framing about the size and shape of an outhouse was covered by worn and torn burlap sacks. The roof of the structure was pyramid shaped, and was also covered with burlap. At the apex, a galvanized steel pipe poured a continuous stream of water so that it flowed equally on the four sides and down the rectangle structure. A hinged side, also covered with sack, could be opened like a door, allowing food and perishables to be hung within or laid on the ground of the creek bed that had been leveled with creek rocks.

The evaporation of the spring water soaking through the burlap by capillary action created a "cool" interior regardless of the outside summer temperatures.

Nonno was amazed at how cold the hams and produce and jarred goods felt to the touch. The pipe supplying the water went further upstream to a man-made pond from which the water flowed by gravity down and over the sack "cooler," then resumed its flow downstream. Constant dampness had rotted the framework and much of the burlap. Ann depended heavily on this cooler to keep meats and butter and other staples cool and fresh. Beverages in bottles, allowed to sit in the stream itself, were downright "cold," since the brook was fed by melting snows in the nearby hills. The simplicity of the structure fascinated Nonno, and its operation made sense. Ann started ripping off the old burlap and pointed to the rotted frame members she was hoping Nonno could fix. Behind the cabin there were tools: saws, shovels, etc., and 10- to 12-foot lengths of redwood two-by-fours. The better part of the morning, Nonno tore down the old cooler and matched the framework with new lumber. Ann sewed new burlap feed sacks together that would eventually be tacked to the new wood frame.

It was early afternoon when Ann turned on the faucet over the pyramid top. She re-hung and replaced her meats and preserves. Though Nonno figured how the cooler kept away flies and insects, he couldn't imagine what deterred bears or raccoons, attracted by the food smell, from tearing the cooler apart. That contingency was covered by a series of heavy iron-barred grates that once surrounded the cooler like a fence. Nonno saw the grates scattered and half-buried in the underbrush. Figuring his job was not done, he began to pull out the grate panels to re-fence the area, but Ann said, "No. My husband can do that—you have helped me enough." From a wooden box she had replaced in the cooler, she pulled out a jar of brandied cherries and a wrapped package of meat labeled "venison steaks." It appeared Ann expected to entertain her guest again for dinner, and Nonno wasn't about to protest, but tomorrow he must leave — however painful it was to have to forego the hospitality.

* * *

Nonno was no stranger to temptation. He had faced it in France, while crossing the Atlantic, and at the brothel in New Orleans, yet through it all he had managed to remain faithful to Elisa.

Now, in the middle of a wooded wilderness, primal urges preoccupied all thinking, because he could not ignore the fact that his hostess was young and beautiful in his eyes; she manifested an apparent loneliness and caring that nurtured Nonno's imagination. As Nonno crudely put it, any man can fantasize under what circumstances he'd drop his pants. This encounter was pushing the ideal.

The invitation to stay for another meal had been punctuated by Ann's change of clothes. Her bib overalls gave way to more feminine attire, and Nonno described it as a flowing pleated skirt with a drawstring peasant blouse. It had to have made an impression, for I never knew Nonno to remember, let alone describe, clothing on anybody. He even remembered that Ann's hair had been combed out to shoulder length. But most disturbing was that he found it hard not to stare at Ann's cleavage. Her movements as she readied the evening meal convinced Nonno she wore no undergarment.

"Give me your shirt," said Ann. "I'll wash it for you and it will be clean by the time you leave tomorrow." Nonno didn't understand. Ann pointed to the wash tub outside and the washboard in it. She then physically began to unbutton Nonno's shirt. "I clean," she tried again, and Nonno got the message. His days on the road — and what with wood chopping and carpentry on the cooler — had taken their toll. Nonno also removed his undershirt and Ann took it, jokingly holding her nose, agreeing that it, too, needed laundering. While Ann tended to the washing, Nonno sponged by an outside faucet next to the cabin. He was surprised the water was warm, then realized the warmth was provided by a coiled hose on the roof of the cabin that was exposed to the southern sun. The warm water didn't last long, as the cold water from the spring pushed through the hose. If used sparingly, the crude solar system worked for a few minutes.

Nonno dried himself and tidied up. Still stripped to the waist, he entered the cabin. Ann had already started the stove and fireplace; however, she had gone upstairs. Nonno instinctively sought out the five-string guitar and began to improvise some chord passages. Ann soon emerged from her bedroom, transformed. Her hair was still down and loose, but held back on the sides by two mother-of-pearl combs above her ears. A different skirt was shorter, to about mid-calf, and flat slippers accented attractive ankles. The peasant blouse was a hand-sewn print like the one Nonno had admired the day before. This one was a bit thinner and tighter fitting — at least Nonno thought it was.

The guitar playing stopped as Nonno watched Ann descend the stairs. His staring was interrupted when Ann handed him the jar of brandied cherries to open. The jar lid had corroded tight, but Nonno's strength knew no bounds at this moment. Ann poured two healthy shot glasses of the brandy and then added four cherries into each drink. For toothpicks, she broke off two straws from the upper bristles of the kitchen broom.

In the warmth of the fire, as dusk darkened the nearby trees, Nonno and Ann sipped brandy — said "*Salute*" many times, and just smiled at each other's company, careful to keep their mutual emotions in check.

Nonno's self-consciousness made him fiddle with the guitar. Ann got up once or twice to set the table and prepare the venison steaks she had marinated with wild rosemary and sage leaves.

The warmth and odor from the baking bread plus the flickering light from the fireplace, to say nothing of the effects of the brandy, cast a dreamlike spell. Nonno was having difficulty remembering his fingering on tunes he once knew subconsciously. Nonno confided to me when I was old enough to appreciate the circumstances that, in his mind's eye, Ann's breasts were getting bigger by the moment. Finally, he thought he must dart outside to sober his libido in the cool of the evening air.

It's debatable whether Ann was cognizant of the extent to which she was "bothering" Nonno. Outside the cabin Nonno was thinking to himself, "She's asking for it."

"Ottorino," she called out (this was the first time she had called him by name), "Where are you? You'll catch cold out there."

Nonno reluctantly re-entered the kitchen and his bare chest brushed past those eager bosoms in the constriction of the doorway. Ann did not attempt to move, nor did she resist the intimacy. Nonno, with his last ounce of self-control, proceeded to his chair sweating frustration from every pore.

The sizzle of the venison steaks seemed to echo the sizzle of two young bodies yearning for each other, and then a curious thing happened. As if in a twinge of remorse, Ann burst into audible crying and ran upstairs to her room, thoroughly distraught.

Nonno didn't know what to make of the behavior, nor how to deal with it, because of his language limitations. He rummaged through his knapsack of personal items and took out Elisa's picture and a small one of Renato. Cautiously but tenderly he ascended the steps and knocked at Ann's bedroom door. As she opened it she cried, "I'm sorry," and threw herself in his arms, clutching his neck and allowing her tears to drench his naked chest.

"You very lonely," said Nonno helplessly. "Me lonely too." And he showed the two snapshots to Ann. "*Mia moglie e figlio.*" Ann held the pictures, being careful not to soil them with her tears.

"I'm so sorry, Ottorino," she said. "You are such a good and kind man. I am sorry if I acted selfishly." She set the pictures down and took out a clean shirt from what had to be her husband's dresser. "Please put this on," she said. She in turn put on a loose-knit sweater, and hand in hand the two returned to their cooking venison steaks. Ann wiped her tears intermittently. Nonno put the snapshots back in his pack — and the crisis seemed over.

They ate in silence as Ann sniffled and both fought to regain composure. "You good woman," Nonno finally blurted out. "When your husband come back?" Ann just shook her head and didn't answer the question.

Nonno then strummed an aria from the opera *Tosca*, appropriate for the bittersweet sadness of what had transpired. Ann kissed Nonno on the cheek, an antiseptic gesture of thanks, then said, "Goodnight." Nonno was proud of himself; he resisted the kiss, which he could not have done earlier. He responded *"Buona notte"* to Ann, and that was the last he would see of the voluptuous blouse he had come so close to despoiling.

Neither individual slept well. Reciprocal mental telepathy passed through the ceiling and floor separating passions that might have been. Tomorrow morning's parting was going to be painful.

8

Eureka

Ann was cooking at the crack of dawn. Nonno made up his bunk and brought out his knapsack. *"Buon giorno, Ann."*

"Good morning," she replied, but they avoided eye contact.

On the kitchen table Nonno's clean shirts had been folded neatly. An egg carton containing twelve hard-boiled eggs was in a picnic basket, which included pieces of cheese, biscuits, some fruit and other provisions taken from Ann's cooler. As Nonno laced his hiking boots, Ann poured some coffee and buttered some pancakes. "You take, Ottorino," said Ann, "for your travel to Eureka. In two or three days, you will come to Lane's Redwood Flat. Capish? Lane's Redwood Flat," she repeated.

"Si," said Nonno.

"Lumber camp there," said Ann.

"Grazie," said Nonno, and so as not to prolong the agony, Nonno reached for Ann's hand and kissed it in continental style.

They stepped outside together and Ann, noticeably moved, fussed over Nonno as if she was sending a small child to his first day of kindergarten. "Now, you have your food?"

"Si," said Nonno.

"Some money." She slipped a five-dollar bill into his shirt pocket. "I hope I see you again." And she turned and ran for the cabin door, fighting back more tears.

" Addio, Ann," cried Nonno, half raising his hand to wave. He cursed in Italian that he could not verbalize

his gratitude in English. Though tempted to follow Ann back into the cabin, he bravely turned to march up the trail soon enveloped by the ferns. Ann's dog was following him out.

The road had not yet come in sight when he heard Ann desperately yelling, "Ottorino, Ottorino, Ottorino!" He panicked, not knowing what emergency warranted such shouting. Upon whirling around, he saw Ann running pell mell along the trail and slamming past the ferns. She was holding the five-string guitar upon which she had fashioned a rope sling. In the emotion of the parting, she had forgotten to give it to Nonno as her parting token of affection. "*Per te,*" she said in Italian, and as Nonno took it from her, she ran back down the path crying audibly and panting as a result of her sprint.

Nonno stood there fighting the urge to chase and comfort her. The knot in his throat only allowed a weak, "*Ti amo,* Ann," which was drowned in the silence of the forest; he speculated that she probably never heard him.

He never remembered reaching the main road, and his preoccupation of the interlude with Ann carried him northward amid the redwoods until his consciousness snapped him back to reality. By then, the sun was directly overhead.

Two days of pleasant weather and easy walking brought Nonno fifty miles further north. His emotions vacillated between the beauty of the forests and memories he replayed about his encounter with Ann McCloud. The food she had packed and the gift of the guitar were reminders of his regrets that he had not taken advantage of Ann's advances. It felt good, at the same time, that he had resisted, in light of the guilt it would have caused when his thoughts turned to Elisa—yet those breasts beneath Ann's peasant blouse loomed ever larger in the recollecting.

"Damn," he blurted out loud. (He learned and liked this American expletive, because it released tension and had no equivalent in Italian.) "I could have had her." And he kept muttering, "Damn, damn, damn"—angry with himself.

＊ ＊ ＊

In three days Nonno came upon Lane's Redwood Flat. There was no mistaking the smell of smoke from the charred logs, reminding Nonno of the practice of backfiring. He said to the first workman he saw, "Need work—me cutter." Nonno had learned that "cutters" were high on the social order of tasks in the lumber camps. They came behind "sawyers," whose responsibility it was to cut or split the finished planking from any given log. Cutters chopped the huge wedge from the trunks to fell the logs precisely where they were required.

"Gotta talk to the foreman," said the worker, and he pointed to a cabin across the work clearing. At that exact moment, two women exited the cabin giggling. A huge lumberjack, maybe six-three, 250 pounds, followed the ladies; he was buckling his pants.

The worker who had pointed out the cabin to Nonno yelled, "Hey, McCloud, there's a cutter here to see ya."

Nonno knew right away this had to be Ann's husband, but before he could conjure up some kind of introduction, McCloud yelled, "Hey, you with the guitar— that's MY guitar!—and you're wearing my shirt! You've robbed my house!" He sprang at Nonno, pinning him with his excessive bulk to the frame of a disc saw. Nonno struggled to no avail to break free from a choke hold. Even if he could explain his meeting with McCloud's wife, the evidence was overwhelmingly against Nonno in McCloud's eyes. There is no time for reasonable explanations when you are choking to death.

In desperation, Nonno managed to free one hand and retrieve his pocket knife, which he could snap open with his fingers. In a single motion, he could "draw the knife" by brushing it past his side and snap the handle open to reveal the blade with the same speed of later-day switchblade models. Only when Nonno's blade drew a trickle of blood from McCloud's neck under his ear did the latter relinquish his chokehold. Nonno's adrenaline and the accusation of being a thief so infuriated his otherwise peaceful nature, he came within seconds of plunging his knifeblade into McCloud's throat. The further realization that McCloud was cheating on his lovely wife only compounded his anger. Luckily, cooler heads separated the combatants from possible dire consequences.

Coughing from the choke hold, Nonno managed to rattle, "Me no thief. You wife, Ann, give me guitar and shirt. She say you foreman this camp—me need work. I chop wood for Ann. You bad man," said Nonno, pointing to the two prostitutes who had paused to witness the scuffle. Nonno wanted to condemn McCloud's infidelity in front of his peers, but was frustrated by his inability to articulate in English.

"If you touched my wife, I'll kill you," threatened McCloud, trying to reinforce his accusation, but still restrained by several workmen.

"Me no touch her," said Nonno. "Me help her—she good woman—you bad man!" Nonno wanted to say

McCloud didn't deserve such a prize as Ann, but he didn't know how. "I go," said Nonno, and pointing to his shirt and the guitar he yelled, "This mine. Ann gave me. You bad man. Your wife lonely."

Nonno repocketed his knife and backed his way up the dirt road he had entered. It was a close call, he said to me in confidence. "Lucky, I could reach my pocket knife."

As a youngster, I was captivated by trying to duplicate Nonno's switchblade maneuver with a conventional pocket knife. Because he had strong fingers, he could pinch the blade open slightly, on most pocket knives, with one hand. While still holding the blade, he would swing the knife forward, brushing the handle against his hip. This opened the handle on its hinge, allowing his hand to slide back upon it and reveal the menacing blade pointing forward.

The entire sequence was in a single motion, as speedy as the action of a switchblade, but without the audible click.

Nonno and I would have "quick draw" contests when we knew we were each carrying a pocket knife. Arms akimbo announced our intentions. At the count of three, we would go for our knives. In spite of my younger years and so-called faster reflexes, I could never win the draw. Nonno was patient in showing me his technique. I practiced secretly to improve my speed. When I had worked up confidence, I'd surprise him with "one, two, three." He still beat me to the draw and would go off laughing at my frustration.

One day I needed to cut some string, and casually asked Nonno to lend me his knife. I knew he was never without it. It was then I discovered the secret of his superior speed. His knife blade had a broken main spring and opened loosely on its pivot. While I struggled to pinch my blade open, Nonno merely flicked his broken blade open in our quick-draw challenges. I was devastated he had taken advantage. Though we laughed at the deceit, deep down I never forgave him for making me lose all those quick-draw confrontations. I'll admit, I smile every time I use a pocket knife and remember how it pleased Nonno to have put one over on me.

✳ ✳ ✳

Eureka seemed dank and gloomy to Nonno—a far cry from the more pleasant weather he had experienced the last week of his trek north. Hitching rides on logging trucks was easy as they returned empty from the lumber mills as far south as Ukiah and Garberville.

The constant drizzle gave the town a depressing feeling, but Nonno detected the activity of commerce. He couldn't imagine why his sister Santina and Pellegrini opted for such a forlorn destination. But he got an inkling of the prosperity as he sought directions to the waterfront. Santina had alluded in earlier correspondence to Pellegrini's ability as a fisherman. So Nonno figured this was as logical a place as any to start looking for Santina.

His ability to distinguish ethnic features became an asset. He could spot a Sicilian at fifty paces. Hence he had no hesitancy in approaching them to make inquiries, even though the Sicilian fishermen found his Tuscan dialect foreign to their ears.

"Might you know about a recent arrival called Pellegrini?" Nonno asked. Most shook their heads. Few asked why he wanted to know. A suspicion and fear of strangers was characteristic of this tight-lipped society. But Nonno persisted; his tact and good nature won the trust of one fisherman who said, "There's a Pellegrini on Gunther Island. Fishes from a skiff for crab." The man pointed out to the middle of Eureka Bay.

"How can I get there?" asked Nonno.

"No need," replied the fisherman, pointing to the water. "Someone's rowing in from there now. Could be Pellegrini—or a person who knows him."

Nonno strained his eyes at the skiff and figured at the rate of progress landfall could take about half an hour. The oar strokes seemed weak though steady, but hardly those of an experienced boatman. But then Nonno's heart pounded a bit faster as the figure got closer to shore. It couldn't be, he thought. It had to be! "Santina?" he yelled, through cupped hands. The figure stopped rowing and stood up to scan the shoreline.

"*Soscio?*" she yelled back.

"*Si, si,*" said Nonno as he ran to the point on the beach where the skiff would land.

Santina almost upset the skiff as she lunged to the beach, oblivious of wetting her shoes and skirt. Her brother was knee-deep in the bay surf when they embraced amid tears, fog, ocean spray, and the curiosity of onlookers, who realized these two must not have seen each other for a long, long time.

Conversation between brother and sister was nonstop. What, when, and how questions ran rampant as the two played catch-up about the years they had not seen each other. Santina almost forgot she had come to shore for groceries and provisions. Nonno helped carry bags of stuff back to the skiff to be rowed back to Gunther Island.

As Nonno rowed, Santina filled him in about Pellegrini, who was out fishing. How their trek across America paralleled the experiences Nonno had endured. How loneliness and fear plagued her pregnancy. How the aborted birth affected her relationship with her husband and how they reconciled. How they ended up on Gunther Island out of despair. They were literally squatters, referred there by another fisherman also down on his luck, who took pity on Pellegrini and told him about the abandoned dwelling on Gunther Island.

Santina was noticeably embarrassed and ashamed of the dilapidated household as she showed Nonno where to put his things.

"That's not your guitar," she said.

"I know," said Nonno. "Mine was stolen in San Francisco. It's a long story."

"We haven't been here long," said Santina apologetically.

"I gathered that," said Nonno. "I found your house in San Francisco, and your landlady told me you came north."

"How'd you get here?" asked Santina.

"I walked," said Nonno, "worked my way up. It's been many months."

"Fishing was bad in San Francisco before the quake," said Santina. "Pellegrini was told crabbing was better here in Eureka. We're making a little money—and so can you." Her voice turned optimistic.

"When will Pellegrini be back?" asked Nonno.

Santina answered, "Actually, any time now. I know you two will like each other."

Pellegrini climbed the catwalk from his boat, a peacoat slung on his shoulder. A handsome man, thought Nonno, as he sized up his brother-in-law. The two smiled and extended their hands. "They told me on shore you were here," said Pellegrini.

"That's what they told me," said Nonno. The two men got acquainted as Santina busied herself for the evening meal, which included a precious bottle of red wine to celebrate their reunion.

Later Santina brought out letters she had saved from Elisa, and Nonno devoured their contents. He resolved he would learn all about fishing as fast as Pellegrini could teach him. The letters from Elisa reminded him how much he missed her, how much he had missed seeing his baby son, Renato. Oh, how he wanted to accelerate his family coming to America to join him.

Pellegrini and Nonno were rowing the skiff at dawn. "First," said Pellegrini, "we fish for *Moccara*" (whitebait). "This is the bait we use for the crab rings."

Nonno was a fast learner and wanted to succeed. The men doubled Pellegrini's usual haul of Dungeness crabs the first day. Pellegrini handed Nonno $2.50 in gold, his share of that day's catch. "You have Santina to care for," said Nonno. "I can't impose on your earnings. How do I get my own boat to start fishing?"

"You can rent one," said Pellegrini. "That's how I got started. Fifty cents a day will get you a waterlogged skiff until you can afford your own. You can use some of my equipment. I have some spare traps."

Nonno's first day alone repeated the pattern Pellegrini had taught him. By himself he earned $5.00 that day. He gave $1.00 of it to Santina, 50¢ for the boat rental, and $3.50 went into the "Elisa jar"—his first contribution from fishing for his family's passage.

Nonno's creativity accentuated his prowess as a fisherman. He studied the tides and inquired about the breeding habits of the Dungeness crab. He talked constantly about fishing with the veteran Sicilians who otherwise jealously guarded their fishing secrets. But Nonno won their confidence with stories of how he was working to bring his family from Italy. The Sicilians identified with his good nature and intentions. They told him how crabs were more plentiful outside Eureka Bay. But rowing would take too long, and a small boat was dangerous in the open ocean. "But I can modify the rented skiff," thought Nonno. With Santina's help, he fashioned a latine sail from old canvas discarded in the Gunther Island dwelling. Using two eucalyptus saplings for booms, Nonno fashioned the triangular sail. He mounted it on a short mast he tied to the bow of his rented skiff. This rigging halved the time it took him to get his bait in the morning and then reach the crab beds near the mouth of Eureka Bay. It was still too dangerous to enter the open sea where the Sicilians ventured in motor boats, but Nonno's daily catch in pounds increased. He began sharing his technique with Pellegrini, who now became the student. Nonno also devised two removable levers clamped to the gunnels of the skiff amidships. From these, lines were tied to the tiller yoke, which permitted Nonno to steer and sail by "kicking" the levers with his feet, leaving both hands free to bait, lower and raise his crab rings, and thus increase productivity.

In three months, Nonno had saved enough to buy a larger used skiff from a local boatyard. His sail rig and tiller levers became an integral part of his new boat and inspired other crabbers within Eureka Bay.

"Elisa's jar" was filling faster, but there were constant "withdrawals" for crab nets, equipment, clothing, and "rent" to Santina when Pellegrini took ill and could not fish. Stamps and stationery were a significant expense as Nonno wrote more and more to Elisa to bolster her hopes. He sometimes had to send money for Renato's schooling. It seemed the harder he fished, the more were the demands on "Elisa's jar," keeping it from filling to shorten the time until she and Renato could book passage.

Nonno soon realized that he could not increase volume, fishing from a skiff, even with his sailing enhancement. The Sicilian fishermen, with their motorized Hicks engine hulls, were hauling in three to four times what Nonno could do on his best days. He needed a bigger boat and motor, and he lamented about this to Santina and to Elisa in his letters. The required investment would have cleaned out "Elisa's jar." To fight the temptation, Nonno sent what dollars he had saved to Elisa with instructions not to spend them. The problem, pure and simple, was how to obtain and afford a motor boat.

✳ ✳ ✳

Nonno's success and ambition had not gone unnoticed by the other crab fishermen, and one of them propositioned Nonno one morning on a bait run. His name was Tappo, and until Pellegrini's and Nonno's arrival, the only other Toscano or non-Sicilian crabber on Eureka Bay. Nonno had heard about Tappo but had never met him.

"I don't like Pellegrini," said Tappo, without any elaboration, "but you are different." Nonno didn't rise to the criticism. He remained silent. "I like the way you fish," Tappo continued. "I can get us another boat. When I teach you what I know, we can both make more money.

I'll buy the boat, you fish it—and we split sixty-forty. The sixty percent you'll earn is more than you are making now."

Nonno was sharp in math, and he quickly calculated his 60% based on the average he knew the Sicilians were making.

"Tell you what," replied Nonno. "I'll give you 50% of the daily take if at the end of one year, the boat is mine."

Tappo had the advantage of knowing the price of the boat. Nonno was shooting from the hip. But his desire to own his own boat was strong, and his counter-offer was an opportunity he must seize upon if Elisa and Renato were ever going to join him. "Done," said Tappo. "See you tomorrow morning at the gas pumps."

It was a Monterey hull, about 25 feet, with a clipper bow. A one-cylinder Hicks engine with a flywheel provided the power. A magneto and battery jars fired the cylinder. The hull was about five years old. There was no pilot house, but the equipment included trolling poles, nets, crab ring traps, lines, and assorted hardware Nonno recognized to be in good condition.

Tappo was adjusting the idle on the engine. The putt-putt firing of the lone cylinder was erratic, depending on the compression and the spark advance. To Nonno, the engine sounded like a symphony. To Tappo's experienced ear, it needed adjustment.

Both men seemed excited as they pulled out into the bay on their shake-down cruise. The rest of the day, Tappo showed Nonno the use and purpose of everything on board. By nightfall, they had even caught a few crabs. Tappo pointed out likely fishing sites they would explore in the weeks to come. Nonno was motivated. In three days, he felt confident he could solo. On day four, he followed Tappo's boat past the Eureka Bar. They fished within sight of each other and fostered a professional friendship that turned into great camaraderie in their later years. Nonno never pursued why Tappo didn't like Pellegrini—and consequently didn't make much of his partnership arrangements in discussions with Santina. All Nonno cared about was that "Elisa's jar" was filling up, and by next crab season, he would own the *Giordano Bruno*. The name he chose for his boat was in honor of an Italian patriot and follower of Garibaldi, who liberated the old Italian City States into the contemporary democratic reform of the current Italian government.

The name was a political statement by Nonno, not unlike those on bumper stickers, but only Nonno knew its significance. The real Giordano Bruno could hardly have been flattered having his name painted on the stern of a crab boat somewhere in America in a harbor called Eureka. But there it was—duly recorded with the U.S. Coast Guard by Tappo, who relinquished title to the boat to Nonno as he had promised. In retrospect, the year had passed quickly, and Nonno was looking forward to some real income to hasten the day of Elisa's arrival.

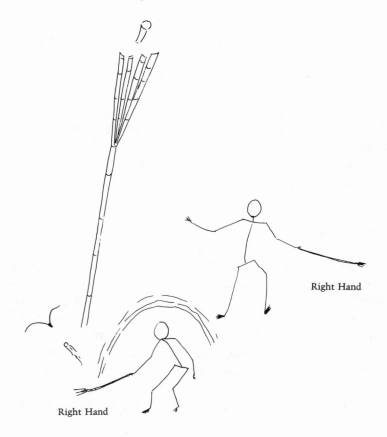

Right Hand

Right Hand

Bamboo throwing stick. *One end of cane would be split four ways, into which you would press a pear-shaped rock or lead pellet melted to the desired shape. With practice, the projectile could travel 100 yards or more, depending on the tension of the split ends.*

Nonno would use this on his fishing boat to scare away seagulls that would dive after his bait. The idea was not to hit the bird, but to force it to veer off its dive until the bait had time to sink to trolling depth.

9

The Surprise

It had not been easy for Elisa. Supporting a small child and the stigma of an absentee husband didn't bode well in Bientina. Gossip persisted that her husband had abandoned her; he was just stringing her along and would never send for her and Renato. Sometimes Elisa even believed it.

Renato was almost six years old now and entering school. He was a bright and delightful child. Elisa read him his father's letters and showed him the latest snapshots from America sent by his aunt, Santina. Elisa, in turn, sent what pictures her meager earnings afforded back to Ottorino to remind him of a son he barely knew.

Added to the scorn from her parents for having married Ottorino ("who ran off") was the prejudice of the community against a single parent, not widowed.

Elisa had to resort to domestic jobs in households when she could find sympathetic employers. She spent time doing piece work weaving linens on hand looms. Her skill in knitting and crocheting supplemented a limited income. Often she was forced to dip into Ottorino's passage money that was earmarked for her fare to America.

Nonna's (grandma's) younger sisters, Maria, Victoria, and Emilia, provided what little empathy and understanding Nonna could count on. They met and socialized secretly to provide comfort and assistance with "hand-me-down" clothing for Elisa and Renato. A gratuitous *lira* was occasionally pressed into Elisa's hand, and Elisa felt both grateful and guilty taking charity from her sisters, who could ill afford it themselves.

Nonna was sustained in her waiting by several arguments. She knew Ottorino loved children and would do almost anything to see his son—including returning to Italy if his efforts failed in America. Ottorino did write, and his expressions of genuine love made Nonna want to believe her waiting was not in vain.

Nonno's income appeared to be gaining strength. She measured his resolve by the slight but perceptible increase of his remittances for the day she could join him. Her greatest comfort came from her correspondence with Santina. Here was a third person's account of what Ottorino was doing, and her sister-in-law would surely not extol Ottorino's efforts and fidelity if it were not true. Elisa could let her hair down and vent her frustrations with Santina, confide in woman-to-woman talk. Santina had since given birth to Lily, her first daughter and cousin to Renato. Letters spoke of the day their children could play and grow up together.

Elisa kept abreast of information about travel to America. She read promotional ads and schedules of the shipping lines and confirmed costs from travelers who had returned from America. She had passport and Italian government regulations memorized, and would cringe when she heard about discount travel packages because she could not take advantage of them.

She became more disillusioned when some cousins (the Nuti family) and Silvio, Ottorino's younger brother, announced their intention to depart for America. But she was determined in her waiting. "Renato and I will get to America if we have to swim," she would say— but down deep, the reality of six and a half years of delay deepened her despair.

The Surprise

Around this time, my great-grandfather, Pietro Guerrazzi, Elisa's father, passed away at age 93. His legacy included some lands inherited from generations before and which would accrue to his widow. Curiously, his will designated a pro-rata share of the *podere* equally to his surviving six children, of which Elisa was one.

"I'll never see my share," complained Elisa to her sisters and brothers, Guido and Julio. "Please buy my part. I can use the money to hasten my departure for America to join my husband."

Nonna's brothers were against it. Besides, no one had any cash, and selling Elisa's one-sixth share was unthinkable. But her sisters took it upon themselves to help Elisa out of her misery. They mortgaged the *podere* for a sixth of its value. They imposed upon themselves, and over their brothers' objections, the burden of paying off the debt plus interest toward an eventual five-way split of the estate that excluded Elisa.

This meant Elisa would get her money now, an act of compassion she never forgot, and for which she remained beholden to her sisters the rest of her life.

The accumulation of Nonno's remittances plus this windfall barely bought third-class fare on the steamer *Rex*, which was destined to leave Naples for New York in the fall of 1911. Elisa confided her departure plans to Santina with strict instructions not to reveal her intentions to Ottorino until she and Renato were safe in San Francisco.

By chance, Nonna's timing coincided with Silvio's independent decision to emigrate to America. Silvio was encouraged by the Nuti family, cousins who had already established themselves in San Francisco. The Nutis would settle in the outer Mission district of San Francisco to engage in truck farming there and in Colma.

91

Enlarged snapshot of Nonno, which he mailed to Elisa in Italy when he began fishing in Eureka. Circa 1910.

Silvio let his sister Santina know that he was coming to San Francisco to stay with the Nutis. In private correspondence, Silvio confided to Santina that Elisa and Renato were planning to join Nonno and, if at all possible, Elisa wanted to surprise him.

Santina kept all these proposed plans to herself to protect Ottorino from any contingency that might disappoint him. The Nuti family, Silvio and Santina became "co-conspirators" in the hope of surprising Nonno with the arrival of his loved ones.

✳ ✳ ✳

Santina became a nervous wreck. She had heard from her brother Silvio that Elisa and Renato had reached San Francisco. Their stay with the Nuti family would be no longer than it would take to book passage on a steamer that ran regularly between San Francisco and Eureka and points north to Seattle.

"I got a letter from Silvio," said Santina one morning over breakfast. "He's hoping we get the chance to see each other."

"Terrific," said Nonno. "Is he coming north?"

"No," said Santina, "but he would like us to meet someone who traveled with him and who will be arriving in Eureka by coast steamer." Pellegrini caught Santina's wink as she pretended to read this information out loud for Nonno's benefit. Pellegrini was in on the surprise.

"When's this guy coming?" asked Pellegrini.

"Day after tomorrow," said Santina, still scanning the open letter.

Pellegrini said, "Damn, that's the day I've got to see about signing up as a crew member on a purse seiner."

Nonno knew Pellegrini wasn't making this up. Pellegrini had tired of fishing for crabs, and he and Nonno had been discussing the pros and cons of sardine fishing from large trawlers. Demand for fish meal was making sardine fishing lucrative, and Pellegrini wanted in on the action.

"Ottorino, would you mind going with Santina to meet this person? I can't see her going to dockside alone to meet a stranger."

"Sure," said Ottorino, "Tappo and I were thinking of working on our boats that day anyway. It'll work out."

The coast steamer's arrival was always of interest in Eureka. It brought people, commerce, news from its ports of call, and once it brought an amusing disaster when its drunken pilot hit the Eureka pier head on, splintering it to smithereens and grounding the steamer's bow into the shore. No one was injured in the accident, but damage was extensive. Civilians still gathered when the steamer docked, half-hoping for a repeat performance.

Santina spotted Elisa and Renato on the exit deck from which a gangplank would lead them to the pier. Since she was supposed to be meeting a "stranger," she didn't wave. Ottorino had seated himself on a piling, scanning through a newspaper to keep from being bored.

"*Babbo*," said a young voice, "*sono Renato*." Nonno looked up from his paper. His gaze upon the figure before him was one of utter disbelief. He glanced quickly where he knew Santina was, and she was standing there, smiling through tears. From the corner of his eye, he recognized Elisa standing back about twenty paces from where she had encouraged Renato to address his father. As if in a dream, Nonno remembers levitating toward Elisa, taking her in his arms while struggling to feast his eyes on both Renato and his wife. At the same time, he resented that Santina had orchestrated the surprise of his life.

Everyone was speechless. Three adults just stood on the Eureka pier, crying through their smiles at each other. Renato had picked up Nonno's pipe, which the latter had dropped in the excitement. Nonno released his embrace from Elisa to pick up his son, who was holding the pipe. "He's beautiful," said Nonno finally. "Bigger than I ever imagined."

"Why didn't you tell me?" Nonno addressed the question to both Santina and Elisa at the same time. It was the first of a million questions as the foursome, arm in arm, headed to claim Elisa's trunk and then return to Gunther Island.

Renato was excited about boarding a skiff and seeing his father row. Like all children, he asked, "When are we going to get there? I'm hungry."

The Surprise

It took several days for Nonno and Nonna to unravel the reality of the impact to their lives. So much to share — so much catching up to explain.

"I could have prepared for her coming," Nonno kept lamenting.

"You'd have worried yourself sick," insisted Santina.

"You were in on this too," Nonno accused Pellegrini.

"So was your brother Silvio," said Pellegrini in a weak defense.

There were parties and rejoicing. Santina invited Tappo and other fishermen to meet Ottorino's family. For the first time, Renato heard his father's talent on the guitar. Santina sang every song in Nonno's repertoire. The partying lasted for days.

Santina was fond of saying in later references to the arrival that Renata, Nonno and Elisa's second child, was born nine months and ten seconds from the day Elisa landed on Gunther Island.

* * *

Understandably, Nonno had to take some time off from fishing. There was just too much to tend to. Carpentry and clean-up had been on indefinite hold on Nonno's side of the dwelling. He began fixing, painting and partitioning off a separate space for Renato.

Elisa had to get used to the routines heretofore established by Santina and her family. Learning to row a skiff was paramount among Nonna's priorities. This skill allowed her the only privacy to escape from island confinement or to shop on the mainland.

Renato accompanied his cousin Lily to school; he too had to learn to row and, when the tides were right, to cross the channel. Santina enrolled him in the third grade based on age. The school put him in the second grade until he could become proficient in English. By the end of the first semester, they had skipped him to the fourth grade.

Adjusting to school wasn't all that smooth. Older boys dared Renato once to smoke some cigarettes, and he did so in the fourth grade classroom. Both Santina and Elisa were summoned to nip this indiscretion in the bud.

Elisa had never questioned why the dwelling on Gunther Island was built on stilts and pilings about six feet high above ground. It was so inconvenient, she thought, to have to negotiate a rickety ladder to a narrow catwalk barely twelve inches wide. On occasion, Renato would be greeted by Santina's dog when he came home from school, and invariably the dog's enthusiasm toppled Renato off the catwalk into the mud flats below. Elisa would be furious.

One morning Elisa was awakened by the lapping of seawater beneath the floorboards of her bedroom. Infrequently, high tides totally submerged Gunther Island. Elisa became so frightened she burst into Santina's bedroom screaming they were all going to drown. She was reassured, to her embarrassment, that all was normal, but she never lived down her fear. After this incident, she confided to Nonno, "How long must we live here? I never imagined living conditions would be so primitive." Nonno tried reassuring her the situation would be temporary. For the first time, he began feeling the pressures of a head of household. He had a son in school and another child on the way. Santina also confided to Elisa that she was pregnant again. Two growing families would find it difficult co-existing on Gunther Island.

Ottorino's preoccupation with domestic problems

The Surprise

was not improved when one morning Tappo told Nonno, "We've got a problem. The Sicilians are saying that the crabs have moved south to Bodega Bay and beyond toward Santa Cruz."

"I can see it in the reduction of our daily weights," agreed Nonno. "In fact, that's the reason Pellegrini is thinking of going on the purse seiners for sardines."

"I won't do that," said Tappo, "I'm a crab fisherman. If I were you, Bianchi, I'd consider taking your family to San Francisco to fish out of there. Eureka is no place for your wife and children."

"How much time before you leave, Tappo?" asked Nonno. "You know the coast and I don't. I'd have to follow you south, if I choose to leave."

"The weather is best in another month," answered Tappo. "This should give you time to talk it over with Elisa."

Elisa was delighted to hear they might be leaving. Santina's company was gratifying, but Nonna was thinking ahead to the time her second baby would arrive. She would much rather be in San Francisco with her cousin Natalina Nuti. She knew there were doctors and hospitals in San Francisco, and that gave her peace of mind, should there be complications at birth.

Nonno worried how to get his wife and child to San Francisco. Following Tappo down the coast with a pregnant wife and small son on board was out of the question. The open ocean was more of a risk than Nonno wanted to take.

Santina inquired about railroad schedules going to San Francisco. A return trip by coast steamer for Elisa and Renato was ruled out because of the cost. The truth of the matter was that Nonno couldn't even afford the one-way train tickets for his wife and son.

Permission to stay with the Nutis had been confirmed. "You are welcome here until you find work," wrote Natalina. This eased Nonno's mind about moving south, but travel money still posed a problem. All cash reserves had been exhausted on home improvements. Nonno couldn't borrow from Pellegrini because his contract on the purse seiner didn't assure him of his pay until the sardine catch was sold. Nonno was reluctant to ask for money from the Nutis, for after all, they were going to house him and his family in San Francisco.

Nonno announced one morning he was going to go to the lumber mill on Samoa, in Eureka Bay (still the site of the Georgia Pacific pulp mills). Freight trains hauled lumber from there to the Bay Area. Perhaps he could finagle a ride south for Elisa and Renato. It wouldn't hurt to investigate the possibilities. Santina gave him little encouragement for success.

When Nonno entered the office of the train dispatcher at the mill, he was shocked to hear a feminine voice say, "Ottorino, what are you doing here?" Nonno turned to feast his eyes upon a well-dressed woman he hardly recognized. It had been well over a year. It was Ann McCloud!

10

Back to San Francisco

Nonno glanced left and right, worried Ann's husband might be with her. He didn't relish a repeat confrontation. Ann sensed his anxiety and reassured him. "He's not here; he's been transferred north to Oregon, and I am on my way to join him. I'm sorry about what happened to you at Lane's Redwood Flat."

"You happy?" blurted Nonno.

"Yes," she said, "we've worked things out. Did you find your sister?" asked Ann.

"*Si,*" said Nonno, and he pulled from his wallet snapshots of Elisa, Santina and Renato. "Must go to San Francisco," said Nonno. "Crab fishing no so good. *Mi* wife expecting *bambino.*" Nonno extended his hands in front of him for emphasis. "She must take train. No money. Me try to get ride for them to San Francisco."

"I can help," said Ann. She went to an attendant seated behind a desk. Nonno could not understand the conversation, but he saw Ann sign a paper. The next thing he knew, she handed him a railroad pass for two, good for thirty days.

Nonno was speechless. Ann went on to explain that her husband's influence in the lumber business allowed for unlimited railroad travel for him or his dependents. Ann merely signed and requested accommodation for two and gave them to Nonno.

"I still play your guitar—fix string," said Nonno in an attempt to communicate his gratitude. "I never forget you."

"Neither have I," said Ann sadly.

"*Grazie* for the pass. I will pay for it when I get money."

"No need," said Ann as she squeezed his hand. Nonno kissed her square on the lips. That's the least he could do, he thought; even Elisa couldn't object to that as the price for free transportation.

Santina was flabbergasted at the sight of the railroad passes. "Tell me again—who was this lady?"

"A friend I met once," said Nonno. "Just a friend."

Tappo hastened his departure time by two weeks because of favorable weather. Elisa and Renato would use their railroad passes a week later. If all went well, everyone would be united at the Nutis' by month's end.

Silvio, who was staying with the Nutis, was scheduling his move to Santa Clara. The brothers would have a short time in which to see each other. Then Nonno would occupy Silvio's guest room, where Elisa could wait for the birth of my aunt, Renata.

The Pellegrinis suffered mixed emotions at the prospect of Nonno and Elisa's parting. Santina cried, thinking she was forcing her brother out, and she didn't relish being alone again on Gunther Island. Pellegrini's new job on the sardine trawler was working out, however. He promised Santina they could move into Eureka proper before her second child (Paul) was born.

Elisa looked forward to returning to San Francisco to live with her cousin Natalina. She and Renato waved to Nonno and Tappo from the Eureka pier when the two crab boats left in tandem across the Eureka Bar and veered south.

❊ ❊ ❊

Tappo was planning some strategy as he and Nonno entered the Golden Gate. He hailed Nonno to heave to just past Fort Point.

"Listen," said Tappo. "We're going to have difficulty finding a berth at the San Francisco Fisherman's Wharf. Let me do the talking."

The Sicilian fishermen had formed "The Crab Fishermen's Protective Association" in San Francisco a few years earlier in a move to stabilize the price for crab and not be at the mercy of supply and demand, which affected their profits. One of their practices was to withhold daily catches in *vivaii* (live traps). Huge submerged crates at dockside could hold live crabs a reasonable time if the market prices were low. The supply would be doled out when market conditions were more favorable.

A Mr. Farina headed the association, and this "brotherhood" was a pretty close and impenetrable group. The only non-Sicilians on the San Francisco Wharf at that time were Tappo and an Irishman who had married the daughter of a Sicilian fisherman. The latter was still resented by most of the fishermen, who perceived his presence as a crack in their wall of exclusivity. Rumors persisted that the Irishman had married the girl only because he wanted to fish.

Tappo didn't foresee any difficulty joining the association, even though he had been away in Eureka. But he had reservations about whether another Toscano would be allowed into the membership. The downside risk was that Nonno might have to fish out of Sausalito or Oakland or at some less convenient dockage.

Tappo instructed Nonno to kill his motor, and he tossed him a line. "If we go in with you in tow, we've got a better chance of tying up together—until I can find and talk to Mr. Farina."

It was mid-afternoon when Tappo led the *Giordano Bruno* between the clipper bows near Cincotta's Boatworks. A few Sicilians, already in from their day's fishing, waved to Tappo in recognition. But they eyed with suspicion the hull of the *Giordano Bruno*, which didn't look like the other San Francisco hulls since it lacked a pilot house.

"Gotta talk to Farina," said Tappo to a friend. He said it loud enough for the other fishermen to hear. "Can we tie up here for a while?"

San Francisco Fisherman's Wharf
Looking eastward from Cincotta's Boatworks
Circa 1930s

No affirmative answer came from anybody. Tappo just assumed permission and lashed both boats to a piling. Leaving Nonno on board, Tappo clambered to the dock where Tarantino's Restaurant still stands and went upstairs to the offices of the Crab Fishermen's Association to ask for Farina.

Nonno was nervous. It wasn't his nature to sit quietly and have someone plead on his behalf. He pretended to work on his engine under the scrutiny of the nearby

Sicilians whose silence made it clear—this stranger was not welcome.

Nonno lost track of how long Tappo was gone. It seemed forever. Finally, Tappo returned and reboarded his boat.

"I got permission to tie up where we entered the wharf area," said Tappo. "But you are going to have to present yourself before the association directors. I can't promise if they will accept you. We'll have to wait and see."

Tappo and Nonno secured their boats where they were told. Tappo had made arrangements to be with his daughter, who lived in the Marina. Nonno hailed a cab and handed the driver Nuti's address. "Call me at my daughter's house in three days," said Tappo. "Here's her number." The men parted company.

Nonno was grateful to Tappo for helping him in Eureka, for making it possible for him to buy the *Giordano Bruno*, and now for using his influence and reputation to allow Nonno to pursue his livelihood from Fisherman's Wharf.

Elisa and Renato had arrived safely a few days earlier at the Oakland Mole. They were met there by Natalina and her husband, Guglielmo. Silvio, Nonno's brother, was there with his fiancée, Amelia Centoni, Elisa congratulated Amelia, her future sister-in-law.[3] In

---

[3]Silvio and Amelia became the parents of Florence and Italo, who grew up on Homestead Road in Santa Clara on a 75-acre prune orchard. Silvio became a successful prune grower, eventually purchasing his leased acreage. I spent a few summer vacations on this acreage when I was a teenager picking prunes to earn some money. I was a terrible picker, and my back gave out on about the third day. Amelia alternated with Mildred, Italo's

the next few days everyone got to know each other better as they waited for Nonno to arrive.

When Nonno's cab pulled up in front of the Nutis' house, his reunion with Silvio, whom he had not seen for seven years, was heartwarming for both brothers. Nonno liked his future sister-in-law, Amelia. Nuti's children played with Renato. They were all about the same age. At Natalina's insistence, Nonno had to retrieve his guitar from his boat when he returned to the wharf to check on the mooring lines. The Nutis' hospitality was rewarded with Nonno's guitar playing. Elisa and Natalina sang to his accompaniment, reminiscing about the old times in Italy.

Silvio and Amelia left for Santa Clara, promising to invite all to their wedding. Nonno phoned Tappo as they had arranged and reassured him the boats were all right. Tappo told Nonno he would have to appear before the Crab Fishermen's Association at their regular monthly meeting in about a week.

Meanwhile, Guglielmo Nuti, who worked on a truck farm in Colma, had heard from a nurseryman that there would be a tree-planting project along El Camino Real in northern San Mateo County. He asked Nonno, "Would you like some work while you're waiting around? You can earn a few dollars planting some trees."

"Sure," enthused Nonno, and Guglielmo took him one morning to a county workyard in South San Francisco.

---

girlfriend, to rescue me with iced tea as I grasped for prunes in pain. This experience taught me to admire and respect the tenacity of migrant workers.

A brusque foreman was eying a line-up of workers scheduled to dig holes on either side of El Camino to plant saplings called "ironwood," which had been shipped from Australia. We know these trees today as eucalyptus.

"Ever plant trees?" the foreman asked Nonno.

"*Si*, yes," said Nonno.

"Sign here," pointed the foreman without much ceremony. "You men be here tomorrow morning at dawn. The work is going to last three or four days, or until we run out of trees."

Guglielmo delivered Nonno the following morning en route to his own job in Colma. Nonno and about a dozen men boarded a double-team horse-drawn wagon. This wagon was followed by two others carrying supplies, tools and fertilizer. One wagon was carrying a stand of five- to six-foot "ironwood" saplings, their root balls wrapped in burlap.

As the men were directed to dig and plant, the supply and tree wagons made continuous round trips to renew planting loam and trees. Around San Bruno and again in San Mateo, trees and supplies had been pre-delivered.

Attrition among the laborers was high. The work was hard. Shelters for the workers were movable army tents set up each night as the work progressed south. Food was served camp style, reminding Nonno of his days in the lumber camps and on Mount Tam.

The foreman had noticed that Nonno took pains when planting the trees. Nonno removed the burlap carefully and spread the roots, redigging the hole to ensure the root system was properly spread out. He alternated manure and soil when refilling the excavations.

"You, Bianchi," said the foreman, "from now on, you

just plant. The others will dig." This was a break for Nonno, and for the remainder of the week he enjoyed his toil.

After seven days the men were paid in gold. Nonno got a little extra for being the "planter." He could have stayed on, but the day was approaching for his appointment with Tappo and the Crab Board directors . . . and he couldn't miss that.

In later years when we traveled El Camino south to visit the Bianchis in Santa Clara or during the Redwood City years, Nonno always pointed with pride to "his" eucalyptus trees. "See these trees?" he would say. "I planted them."

The stretch of El Camino between San Bruno and San Mateo became known in our family as "Nonno's trees." We used them as a geographic point of reference. People and places were in some direction of "Nonno's trees." "Go past Nonno's trees about one mile, and then turn left," etc., etc.

Nonno often quoted an Italian proverb that said, "For trees to be enjoyed, they must be planted by the grandfather." How truly that proverb applies, when you see the eucalyptus still standing on El Camino Real.

11
Fisherman's Wharf

Mr. Farina sat behind an oak desk at one end of the main meeting room of the Crab Fishermen's Association building. Folding chairs lined the perimeter of the room, which accommodated about thirty members. Directors, seven in number, sat behind a low table in front of Farina's desk. In the center of the room was an empty single folding chair that faced the front. The atmosphere was reminiscent of an Elks or fraternity initiation setting. Flags and Sicilian slogans graced the walls, along with pictures of boats, fish and maritime artifacts.

Tappo and Nonno had been waiting a long time in an outer office. Finally, a man came in and waved Nonno to follow him; Tappo was motioned to stay put. No words were spoken.

When Nonno entered the room, the formality was intimidating. Farina pointed to the center chair. As Nonno sat down in the "hot seat," he removed his hat and held it on his lap. There was a long silence.

"Tappo speaks highly of you, Bianchi," said Farina. "He says you are a good fisherman. Were it not for him, you wouldn't even be here. Are you aware of the rules of this association?" continued Farina.

"No," replied Nonno, "but I heard they are very fair."

"There are those who do not agree with that," Farina said. Nonno remained silent, wishing he had not elaborated on his response.

"Hand Mr. Bianchi our charter," said Farina. One of the directors extended several hand-written pages penned in longhand, and written in Sicilian dialect. "Read this out loud for us," said Farina.

Nonno not only read it, but did so in Sicilian dialect, to the dismay of the members seated along the walls. What Nonno didn't realize was that most present were illiterate. They were surprised to hear the rules themselves, but more surprised to hear Nonno's Sicilian pronunciation.

"You can read and write," said Farina, a bit taken aback by Nonno's fluency with the charter content.

"Tell us, Bianchi, if two fishermen brought in 238 pounds of crab and the price that day was $2.25, how much would each partner get after paying $15.00 for fuel?" No one present except Farina had the math skills to answer this very simple arithmetic problem, but the audience had been primed with the answer by Farina so they could judge Nonno's response.

"Take your time," said Farina, reaching to hand Nonno a pad and pencil.

"$260.25," replied Nonno confidently. He had figured the problem in his head before the pad and pencil ever reached him.

There was a stir by the members. "Very good," said Farina suspiciously, "and how did you arrive at that so quickly?"

"I used *la via del cinque,* subtracted fifteen and divided by two."

Nonno could astound many people and especially my dad and me with number solving by his use of *la via del cinque* or *la via del sete.* My dad and I, having been taught conventional arithmetic in the American school system, could never figure out what he was talking about when he tried to explain his math. A generation and a half later, when my own children were introduced to "new math" and "sets," it became apparent Nonno was using base seven or base five or whatever, to do his mental calculations. His mother had taught him math in this manner, and he could multiply many digits by many decimals with magical speed, all in his head.

Farina's test was not to see how good Nonno was in math. Farina was testing to see if Nonno was literate, because among all the fishermen in San Francisco, Farina and Tappo were the only people who could read and write! The Sicilian fishermen were first-generation immigrants who had never been to school; in southern Italy education was a privilege of the rich. Farina had become president of the Crab Association by default, because he was the only one around capable of writing the charter to which the fishermen had agreed.

Basically, the charter required that a percentage of each fisherman's revenues go to the association to pay Farina a salary and cover expenses. Because the members were illiterate, jealousy and suspicion led to frequent bickering. Many of the Sicilians sold their catches privately, defeating the purpose of the association. Some joined reluctantly.

Mr. Farina stood up, and everyone present followed suit. "You are free to go," said Farina, "but after we dismiss this assembly, I want to see you in my private office."

"How'd it go?" asked Tappo when Nonno returned. "I don't know," said Nonno. "They gave me an easy math problem and made me read their charter. Farina wants to see me after the meeting."

"You're in," said Tappo.

"I'm not so sure," said Nonno.

✳ ✳ ✳

Farina offered Nonno a Toscano cigar from his desk drawer. "We can use you, Bianchi," said Farina with a smile. "You may have noticed the members were pleased with your ability to read and do numbers. I need a secretary who can weigh daily catches, keep track of sales, and disburse proceeds to the fishermen."

"But I want to fish," protested Nonno, "I wasn't seeking a desk job."

"Patience, Bianchi, patience—I'm not finished. You can fish—not only for crab when it's in season, but salmon, striped bass, rock fish, bottom fish (sole, petrale and sand dabs)—this will keep you fishing the whole year. What I want you to do is to be back here by 4:00 every day. Weigh your own catch and then keep the daily records for the rest of our members. From what I've seen, you can do this with one hand. You're perfect, Bianchi, for several reasons: (1) You can fish. Tappo told us that. (2) We know you're honest. [Nonno wondered how he knew that.] (3) You can read and write. (4) You are *not* Sicilian; the members know you have no alliances and you will not try to cheat them. You know, Sicilians do not trust each other!"

Nonno knew Farina wasn't kidding on his last point. The consequences of any misconduct would be cement shoes, even then a strong motivator for straight play when doing business with Sicilians.

Nonno was being hired for two jobs—to fish, under the rules of the association, and to be a bookkeeper during a swing shift at an as-yet-undisclosed salary.

Farina and Nonno shook hands. They went out to see Tappo, who congratulated Nonno. "You'll be great," said Tappo. "Go home and tell Elisa. She will be proud of you."

Elisa was ecstatic. "What will they pay you for the bookkeeping?"

"I don't know," said Nonno. "I didn't ask."

The Nutis were delighted for Nonno as well. "Sunday," said Natalina, "we'll go to North Beach and find you your own flat to rent. Just think, Elisa, you'll be in your own home when the baby arrives."

When Renata was born, it was at 125 Francisco Street, walking distance for Nonno to and from the Fisherman's Wharf.

Nonno was regarded by the Crab Association as today's equivalent of a business computer. He quickly demonstrated his organizational skills and introduced systems the fishermen accepted without question. Merchants soon knew they were dealing with a gentleman of his word and one with principles. Together with Farina's marketing acumen and pricing strategies, the association became a formidable force on the wharf. They began to attract some trawlers with large crews who were forming partnerships to fish for sardines, later for shark liver used in the manufacture of medicines.

This growth brought bigger dues and percentage withholds from daily tonnage of fish for the association. Nonno began fishing less and less, trying to keep up with the record keeping.

He recalled a technique he once had to use for a newly formed partnership of sardine fishermen. Three cousins, former crabbers, sold their boats to buy a trawler for larger sardine revenues. When Nonno weighed and sold their first catch, the cousins didn't know how to divide the proceeds equally while still fulfilling their obligations to the mortgage, upkeep and docking fees on the trawler. Nonno converted their daily sales into half-dollar silver coins and carried this bucket of cash to the cousins. Using a coffee mug, he began dipping into the coins, leveled the top of the cup in a skimming motion to ensure equal volume, and proceeded to apportion cupfuls in sequence to each partner until the supply of coins would not fill the last three cups. "This remainder," said Nonno, "goes for the boat." The cousins were delighted with this solution; they could "see" the equity of the distribution. Nonno was prevailed upon to use the system in other instances to settle payments when the parties could not count currency.

It wasn't until the early thirties that credit began to complicate Nonno's bookkeeping, when he began dealing with hotels and larger restaurants and grocery chains that purchased fish on a wholesale basis.

The Chinese merchants in Chinatown, who were big buyers of fresh fish, always dealt on a cash-and-carry basis. Sometimes Chinese merchants supplied Nonno with the 50¢ coins when they purchased fish because they had heard about his coffee cup disbursal system. The Chinese were also smart enough to figure out that for this accommodation, Nonno often gave them a better price.

✳ ✳ ✳

Nonno's reputation for fairness and honesty sometimes became a burden; he was sought after by fishermen and customers alike to resolve domestic disputes, give his opinion on family life and execute the role of father confessor and part-time psychiatrist. He was asked to read all manner of legal documents the Sicilians

112

required, because they had no one else they would trust. Nonno accepted this responsibility in a good-natured way—partly because it fed his ego, but also because it forced reciprocity and cooperation from the fishermen when prices or policies of the association met with resistance from the members.

While counseling a fisherman one morning, there was a ruckus outside Tarantino's between two Chinese merchants. Nonno's mediation skills were good, but he could not understand Chinese. Nevertheless, he learned the two were squabbling over who had successfully bid on a fresh box of herring. Each was claiming the container was his. Like King Solomon, Nonno was prepared to divide the catch and split it between Chung Wo, whom he knew, and the other Chinese merchant he had never seen before. The adversaries would not accept Nonno's compromise; instead, they began tossing scraps of paper with Chinese symbols upon the ground.

Chung Wo must have been the winner of this game, for he got to "bat" first. The loser stood stoic and compliant up against the building. The winner removed his sling pole from his carrying baskets and, with all his might, at close range, struck his pole across his adversary's forehead. The latter dropped dead at Nonno's feet in a pool of blood from a crushed skull. The survivor picked up his container of herring and marched off in the direction of Chinatown, while Nonno and the fisherman he was counseling stood in shock.

Realizing there was little anyone could do for the bleeding victim, Nonno rushed to call an ambulance and the police. He and other witnesses gave the investigating officers their statements, and the body was taken away.

Nonno never mentioned Chung Wo by name and

he never saw him again until about five years later when Nonno was attempting to collect a delinquent account in Chinatown.

While waiting in the underground labyrinth beneath a market on Grant Avenue to collect some money from a delinquent merchant, Nonno heard a whisper. "Bianchi." Nonno spun around to see Chung Wo, the very same man who had struck the lethal blow many years before.

"Where have you been?" asked Nonno. "You just disappeared."

"Big trouble, Bianchi. Big trouble," repeated Chung Wo. "You good man, you no turn me in."

"I never saw . . . " Nonno started to say, but at this point was interrupted when a Chinese girl delivered a check to Nonno for the full amount of the bill he was trying to collect. Chung Wo bid Nonno goodbye and the two never saw each other again. Nonno wasn't about to interfere with some kind of Chinese justice he couldn't understand. All he knew was that the particular market that was delinquent, where he had seen Chung Wo, paid like a slot machine for the remaining years Nonno sold them fish and until the day Nonno had to leave the wharf and his job.

Illustrated Daily Herald *photo featuring article about Ottorino and crab fishing in San Francisco Bay Circa 1926*

12

Discord

The years on Francisco Street were pleasant ones for Nonno and Elisa. Though luxuries were minimal, the family grew and prospered.

Renato spent some teenage years delivering the Italian paper, lighting the then-gas street lamps in North Beach and ushering at the Palace Theatre on Columbus. He attended Poly High School because his mother insisted he learn a trade, which was the curriculum emphasis at Poly.

Renata attended Sara B. Cooper Grammar School. One day in the third grade, she took ill and her teacher asked for a volunteer to see her home. Beatrice Campi, in the same class, carried Renata home piggyback. These little girls became lifelong friends before they ever knew they would become sisters-in-law by virtue of Beatrice marrying Renato.[4]

Both Renato and Renata were obedient, happy children. My dad enjoyed school and boasted that his surveying class at Poly worked on the actual measurements of Kezar Stadium. Renato also took woodshop at school. One of his shop projects was to design and build a pilot

---

[4]Each was the maid of honor at the other's wedding. Each raised two children. My brother Ray and I and my cousins Lorraine and Jean were all raised like siblings. At this writing, my mom and aunt, in their 80s, are planning their first-ever ocean cruise to Alaska together. The "Gold Dust Twins," as they are affectionately called, have shared the longest relationship of anyone in our entire family.

house for Nonno's fishing boat so that the *Giordano Bruno* would look like the other craft at the wharf.

Whereas most of the Sicilian fishermen built their pilot houses from common lumber that was subsequently painted, Renato purchased some exotic tropical wood called Jenisero. The end result was varnished, making Nonno's boat look like a sport model of the traditional Monterey hull. Nonno was so proud of the pilot house. He bragged how his son had gotten an "A" on his project.

My grandparents also encouraged their children to learn music because this was Nonno's first love. Renato became a pretty good mandolin player with some proficiency on the violin. Renata was given piano lessons because a fisherman friend of Nonno wanted to get rid of an old upright piano.

When the piano was moved to the Francisco Street flat, neighbors helped carry it up to the second floor; however, the piano got stuck when the well-meaning muscle power failed to negotiate the first curved landing on the steps. My Aunt Renata was amused that everyone going up and down the stairs ran their fingers on the keys announcing their comings and goings. She received her first piano lesson standing up on the stairs while the piano was still tilted and stuck on the steps. Practice with family or jam sessions required Nonno and my dad to take positions above or below the piano so Renata could be part of the ensemble. It was months before professional piano movers were hired to get the piano to its designated place in the parlor.

Singing, music, good food (unlimited fresh fish) sustained the hard-working family. Elisa found employment at the Cannery near the wharf and we learned many years later about a surprising coincidence. In

118

group pictures taken of the cannery workers, both my grandmothers were pictured side by side. They had known each other as fellow workers before my mom lost both her parents to the flu epidemic. Both women had known each other, never to realize that their respective children (Renato and Beatrice) would someday marry. You recall in an earlier chapter how my maternal grandfather Campi met Nonno during the earthquake. Both sets of grandparents crossed paths before either knew their respective children would contribute to the melting pot of North Beach Italians.

※ ※ ※

As in most families, anxieties and conflicts were not absent. Elisa dreaded the nights when Nonno was late returning from the sea. Many an evening was spent on Scoma's Pier at the wharf where Nonna and the Sicilian wives peered through fog, hoping to catch a glimpse of the running lights on the boats of their loved ones.

Nonna could detect the *Giordano Bruno* as far as the Golden Gate if the visibility was clear. The green light was ever so slightly lower than the red on the opposite beam, and she had memorized the pattern even when fog obscured the rest of the hull. Nonna and her children would return home when the sighting was confirmed to prepare Nonno's late supper. This was frequent when the weather turned bad in the fall and winter months on San Francisco Bay.

When he was growing up, Renato took every opportunity to go fishing with his father. He learned to love the sea, and aspired to become a sea captain. He spent weekends on the *Giordano Bruno* painting and fixing, sometimes to Nonno's exasperation. But Nonno nurtured his son's interest by teaching him navigation and the rules and lore of his maritime experiences.

My dad's ambition became known to one of his teachers named Prunati, who taught languages at Poly High. Prunati took particular interest in Renato because he was bright and, in Prunati's assessment, wasting his skill on a technical education. Prunati was convinced my dad was college material, and he took it upon himself to assist Dad toward his expressed vocation. He succeeded in obtaining for Renato a four-year scholarship to the U.S. Naval Academy at Annapolis.

This was not an easy accomplishment, especially back then. First of all, Dad was not as yet a naturalized U.S. citizen. College scholarships were rare from a technical school. Congressional endorsements were prerequisites, and here we were dealing with an immigrant family that had never even registered to vote.

Undaunted, Prunati succeeded in getting Renato accepted by Annapolis upon his graduation from Poly High. What Prunati underestimated was the resistance forthcoming from Elisa, who was vehemently against the whole concept.

"No son of mine is going to become a sailor," she stormed. "I didn't come to America so my son could drown in some godforsaken ocean."

Both Nonno and Renato argued and cajoled and tried to point out to Elisa that an honor had been bestowed. But there was no budging Nonna's prejudice against a navy or maritime career. She had an anguished with the wives of the other fishermen; the sea was not to be her son's fate. Furthermore, A.P. Giannini was recruiting Italian bilingual employees for his new Bank of Italy. "Now there is a job," extolled Nonna. The image of the aristocratic European banker, held in high esteem to this day, clouded all logic and explanations about the virtues of Annapolis.

"Forget the navy," she insisted. My father was crushed, disappointed and embarrassed having to face

Crab Fishermen's Protective Association Building
currently the site of Tarantino's Restaurant.
Left to right under the word "CRAB."
Tappo (with hat) Farina (no hat)
Nonno (with hat) Others (not identifiable)
Circa 1932

his teacher, Prunati, with the news he could not accept the scholarship. Prunati prevailed upon Elisa and Nonno personally, but to no avail.

Nonna's mind was made up. To distract Renato from his chagrin, Elisa called Silvio and Amelia in Santa Clara to hire Renato for the summer to work on some tomato acreage. My dad played farmer with reluctance, and unfortunately an early frost killed his entire tomato crop. So much for this diversion, which only reinforced Renato's inconsolability.

In an act of rebellion, Renato signed up with a Merchant Marine recruiter as an apprentice seaman and planned to run away from home. His maiden voyage would be upon a tanker leaving San Francisco for Calcutta, India. Renato made the mistake of sharing his intentions with his sister, Renata. It wasn't long before Elisa was apprised of the proposed escape.

Literally on the day Renato was to ship out, his mother panicked when she realized Renato wasn't bluffing. She called Nonno at work from a neighbor's phone, and in no mean terms demanded that Nonno "kidnap" Renato off that "stupid ship" and get him home immediately.

Nonno had to act. He told Farina he had an emergency, and in the nick of time he escorted Renato down the gangplank by the scruff of the neck back to Francisco Street to face an inquisition that made the one in Spain seem mild.

Elisa finally realized how serious her son's convictions were. An otherwise obedient son had demonstrated total emotional rebellion, and Elisa lacked the psychology to repair this fatal wound to her son's heart.

After the din of reprisals and threats subsided, Elisa resorted to a bribe. "Okay, Mr. Sailor," she cried, "you want to sail? This is what I'll do. You get hired by Mr. Giannini in his new bank. Prove to me you can stay employed for at least six months and I will buy you your own sailboat!"

Nonno was more surprised than Renato. How in heaven's name could they afford a sailboat? This was a crazy solution by a desperate mother, and as Nonno tried to squelch the plan, Elisa pointed to Nonno angrily saying, "And not a single word from you—or I'm packing, taking Renata with me, and we're going back to Italy!"

Nonno knew when to back off. He pushed his hat forward and said, "I'm leaving. I still got six boats to weigh." Renato went to his room, but not before popping his sister on the back of her head for having squealed. Nonna burst into tears, wondering whether her shattered family could ever love and trust again.

There were many silent meals after that. You'd never know there was an instrument in the house, for not a note was sung or played for weeks.

Elisa asked her foreman at work if she could sign up for a second shift. This was how she resolved to keep her promise to buy Renato his boat. In six months she figured she might have a down payment.

Renato applied and went to work as a messenger at the Day and Night branch of the Bank of Italy, which later became the Bank of America. He retired from B of A as a vice president after 43 years, hating every moment. True to her promise, Elisa purchased a used 40-foot yawl, which Renato christened *The Elizabeth* (after his mother) to acknowledge some reconciliation.

With Nonno as peacemaker and nautical advisor, the hard feelings between mother and son finally abated.

But even I could detect, a generation later, the longing in my dad's eyes when he would take me as a child to the San Francisco Marina Greens to watch the ships head out to sea. For Dad, every single one of them was bound for Calcutta, and he imagined he was at the helm of each ship that disappeared west beneath the Golden Gate bridge.

13

Redwood City

When I was born, my folks were living on Lombard Street across from the old Crystal Palace Plunge in North Beach. My grandparents moved in with us as an economy move to pool incomes during the Depression.

Renata had married an immigrant from Lucca, Italy, who had come to America with his brothers. The Guidi brothers owned and operated a grocery in North Beach, where my aunt and uncle met. Guido, my uncle by marriage, took advantage of an opportunity to expand his business by buying property over commercial space at Filbert and Octavia in the Marina Cow Hollow district. My aunt and uncle moved to a flat on Greenwich to be near their "New Rainbow Market." After 50 years, it is still a thriving business run by my cousins and their children.

My parents and grandparents were encouraged by Renata to move to the Marina too so my aunt could be closer to her mother and to my mother. Besides, the Lombard flat was proving too small for two families. In those days, the thought of moving from North Beach to anywhere was as traumatic as the prospect of taking a wagon train to the ends of the earth. Nonno resisted having to leave the proximity of Fisherman's Wharf. My dad had been assigned to the Columbus Branch of B of A at the corner of Green Street, and he enjoyed walking home for lunch. But the arguments of the "gold dust twins" overcame objections. My dad and Nonno could go to work on the F streetcar together. Renata, my mom and Elisa could visit daily. The location of Guido's business amalgamated the family "herding" instinct, which was the key to survival and security for many immigrant families in those days.

This regrouping provided the financial stability for the entire extended family, thanks to my uncle's store. Guido's kindness and generosity came at a good time to rescue Nonno from one of his most traumatic transitions into life in America.

In 1943, Nonno had one of the proudest moments in his life when he became a naturalized U.S. citizen. His business years at the wharf improved his fluency in English, and this gave him confidence to study and pass the examination for citizenship. My grandmother, Elisa, in contrast, refused ever to learn English; consequently, at home, Italian was the language of choice, and I grew up not knowing English until I entered kindergarten at Sherman Grammar School.

Nonno was proud of his U.S. citizenship, but this pride was dealt a devastating blow because of World War II and the events in Europe that allied Mussolini with the Axis cause.

Following the internment of the Japanese after Pearl Harbor, foreign-born Germans and Italians were also considered for internment. No one could have been more patriotic than my grandfather. His effort to attain citizenship proved his allegiance to the country that made it possible for him and his family to survive. Elisa had taken several opportunities to return to Italy to visit her sisters. Nonno steadfastly refused to ever go back. "This is my country," he would say, and he even learned to play that refrain on his guitar.

As the war went on, it was decreed that foreign-born enemy aliens, even if naturalized, could not work near defense or debarkation areas. Pearl Harbor fostered a national paranoia about sabotage; hence, strategic areas such as coastal waters, defense plants, and army installations were to be purged of foreign-born Germans and Italians. This meant Fisherman's Wharf was off limits to the old-time fishermen such as Farina, Tappo and Nonno.

Ottorino's livelihood was taken away from him. If he could not sell his boat, it would be confiscated. The void created in the fishing fleet at the wharf was filled by the native-born children of the Sicilians who resorted to fishing, in an attempt to save their parents' boats. My dad was ineligible for this tactic, for he too was a naturalized citizen and was forbidden from points of debarkation and coastal waters. His feelings were further hurt when, after volunteering to become our block's air raid warden, he was told he was a security risk and could not serve. My mother's bedroom radio, which just happened to have a short-wave band (that never worked) was taken from our home. A sympathetic neighbor who subsequently was selected as air raid warden "stole" the radio back and returned it to my mother.

All of this battered Nonno's self-esteem, and he was justifiably bitter. It was little consolation that he was not singled out for this treatment. His biggest frustration was that familiar geography was off limits, and there was little for him to do.

During this part of my youth I remember spending wonderful days with my grandfather. He took me mushroom hunting out in the Sunset District, which was all sand dunes at the time. He took me to the zoo and taught me all about the animals, their habits, how they hunted, what part of the world they came from. It wasn't until I corroborated some of his facts in my later experiences and reading that I realized how much Nonno knew about animals.

We also attended matinees at the Opera House. I remember seeing Licia Albanese and Enzio Pinza in *Aida*—from the third row center, using Nonno's 7x50 marine binoculars. We had expected to be in the balcony. By some kind of error we were almost in the orchestra pit. With the binoculars, I could count the cavities in the teeth of the chorus. Nonno knew the music of Verdi and Puccini intimately. I grew to appreciate Italian opera, thanks to this enriching exposure.

I also helped Nonno and learned to make "dago red" wine in our basement. This helped him wile away his time and allowed him to invite his fishing friends to taste the results of his labors and to commiserate about their isolation.

At night, Nonno would meet some of his cronies at the bocci ball courts on Filbert and Octavia Streets. Nonna worried about his card playing, and the fact that he wasn't playing his guitar, a sure sign of depression.

Thanks to a suggestion from my uncle Guido, and concurred in by my dad and my Aunt Renata, a plan of action was proposed to buy a "country place" somewhere to house my grandparents and to give Nonno something to do. The plan was also motivated by the fact that my cousin Lorraine suffered from asthma as a baby. Clean country air would be good for her, plus my aunt and my mom could spend summer vacations in such a place and my dad and uncle could have a weekend retreat to enjoy.

Redwood City on the Peninsula (about an hour's drive south before freeways) advertised "Climate Best by Government Test." This sign crossed El Camino Real at Redwood City for many years. Since good climate was a prerequisite because of Lorraine's condition, this seemed like the logical place to look. The realtor's instructions for what was sought were simple: "We'd like the cheapest acreage you can find," said my dad.

A week later, my uncle, dad and Nonno were shown a two-and-a-half-acre parcel. It was half of an original five-acre pear orchard that was for sale on Valota Road on the western edge of Redwood City. Further west was open grassland leading up to the town of Woodside and the Coast Range.

"You can buy this for $2,500," said the realtor. "There's a dwelling, a well and about 200 pear trees. The soil is pure adobe." (Not necessarily an asset.)

North on Valota were a series of Japanese nurseries, inactive because of the Japanese internment. East, across from Valota Road, a large corral complex housed riding and boarding facilities for horses owned by the Olson Nolte saddle works.

My uncle appointed my dad as spokesman to try to negotiate for a lesser price. Nonno's keen eye for the terrain convinced him there was potential for truck farming here. "I like it," said Nonno.

"We'd like to talk to the owner," my dad told the realtor. "But we can't consider more than $2,000." The realtor arranged a meeting with the owner for the same afternoon.

"I'll consider the $2,000 offer," said the seller, "but only on one condition. I have a single, aged German caretaker living on this property. He's somewhat retarded but harmless, a devoted Lutheran who is a ward of his church. He earns a little cash doing menial jobs for his church, and he lives here free. If you promise to accept him and not force him to move, the place is yours for $2,000."

"Can we meet him?" asked my dad.

"Of course," said the seller, and the four men approached the dilapidated dwelling to meet Henry Heinrich, a man in his seventies who always wore a cap. Bicycle shin clips adorned his lower trousers, wrapping them tight about both calves. Several bicycles, his only means of transportation, were strewn in his entry hall. Most of them were used for spare parts for the only bicycle he could ride to and from church. Henry spoke mostly German, very little English, and in either language he constantly talked to himself.

Upon seeing the entourage of men approaching the house, Henry ran away into the pear orchard. "He's a little shy," said the realtor—perhaps the understatement of the day. My dad followed Henry as if he was stalking a rabbit. Henry's bizarre behavior worried both Nonno and my uncle. They were not keen on taking on a weird caretaker, regardless of the price concession. Finally, Dad cornered Henry, and in calm tones tried to assure him no harm would come to him. He could continue to stay on at the ranch—but he could not expect any remuneration other than free housing. Henry never answered. He evaded Dad once more, and backtracked into the house, slamming the door and stumbling over his bicycles.

"I'll talk to his minister," said the seller, "and have him explain to Henry what is going on."

And so it was that the Bianchis and the Guidis purchased "Redwood City" for $2,000 cash, including Henry Heinrich. An imaginary line divided the plot of land lengthwise to designate ownership of the pear orchard. Henry's house was on the Guidi side, and after my Aunt Renata saw it, her first words were, "This *barracca* has got to go!"

* * *

Redwood City (not the town, but the land on Valota Road) never knew what hit it. Reconstruction of Henry's house began one weekend. The side walls were saved intact to provide a two-room cabin or temporary quarters for Henry that ended up being permanent. The original dwelling site provided the foundations for a new, three-bedroom, permanent "Jerry-built" house that grew like Topsy on successive weekends, thanks to the volunteer labor of friends and relatives. Donated second-hand lumber rode the fenders of every family car that ventured to Redwood City. Anyone who had ever thought he was a carpenter (or dreamed of being one) was welcome. People we didn't even know showed up with hammers and saws and picnic baskets just to spend the weekend. The first summer in Redwood City was a construction orgy only a bunch of crazy Italians could have orchestrated.

There were never any plans, nor even sketches. My aunt would say, "I think the kitchen should be here." My mom would add, "And the bathroom should be there." And remarkably, walls appeared and plumbing was routed.

Whenever we needed some real talent, such as an electrician or roofer or painter, Nonno let the word out among his North Beach contacts. These "experts" directed the available workers who happened to show up for work on any given Sunday. A hierarchy not unlike that of a baboon troop developed. Dominant "experts" in their field commandeered their dominion over subservient "gofers" until a "gofer" became a foreman in his field of expertise, and then everybody else dutifully followed those orders. A behavioral psychologist could have written a thesis watching the dynamics of this house being built.

By mid-day, the Redwood City summers got pretty hot. "Okay, let's quit," someone would say, and then the beer, wine and cold drinks preceded the barbecuing. The partying lasted into the balmy summer evenings while everyone discussed what they should tackle the next weekend.

"How about a front porch?" said Scipione Belli. He was my mom's cousin and one of the few who was a professional carpenter. "We've got all this extra lumber."

"Why not?" somebody agreed. Without too much consultation, the next weekend Scipione directed the construction of the front porch which later, everyone agreed, turned out to be the best part of the house.

This organized chaos became a popular sport among relatives and friends who sympathized with the injustice that had been dealt to Nonno, who was deprived of fishing.

"The least we can do is go help Ottorino get started on the ranch." But this battle cry was just an excuse to come and party. My uncle's grocery store supplied most of the food. My aunt, mom and grandmother did the cooking. Visiting wives and kids who accompanied the volunteer help brought salads and pastries plus sports equipment so the children could play in the pear orchard. And this activity didn't stop after the main house was completed. By force of habit, people kept coming to plant lawns, build a 50-foot arbor to seat the guests for the barbecues, help landscape and donate plants as gifts, etc.

Gaspero Cerri, a *paisano* stone mason from Bientina, volunteered to build a brick bread oven from the free cobblestones being ripped up on the Embarcadero in San Francisco. He enjoyed Redwood City so much, he came to add stone steps to the main house, expand the bread oven to include outdoor cooking pits and grills, build an outdoor drinking fountain and wash basin, and eventually a wishing well. We finally ran out of cobblestones because my uncle's pickup truck lost its shock absorbers hauling the cobblestones from San Francisco. We're sure Gaspero would have paved the entire ranch if we hadn't run out of stones.

As the war progressed, rationing impacted what my uncle could sell at his market, and this proved to be the seed of opportunity for Nonno. In addition to vegetable growing, initially intended for family use, Nonno was able to go into truck farming in a big way. Chicken houses were built. (More weekend parties.) Rabbit and pigeon hutches followed, and eventually a horse barn. My uncle could sell all the eggs Nonno produced. The rabbit and squab meat didn't require red rationing stamps. The demand for this homegrown produce exceeded Nonno's ability to produce, and at the height of the war years, Redwood City became a thriving business that preoccupied my grandparents full time, with many chores that even Henry Heinrich found rewarding.

As older pear trees died, Nonno replaced them with walnuts (less care, more revenue). He planted vines from which he made wine. Family connoisseurs acclaimed its virtues. Fruit trees of every variety were planted — cherries, plums, apricots, peaches, apples, figs and quince. They seemed to grow out of spite from the rich adobe soil.

The secret of Nonno's farming prowess was the adaptation of remembered skills he had learned on the *podere* in Italy. "Catching" the soil at the right time to work it was paramount. Adobe cracks and shrinks into cement-like clods in the summer. In winter, the clay content sticks to anything it touches. But its inherent

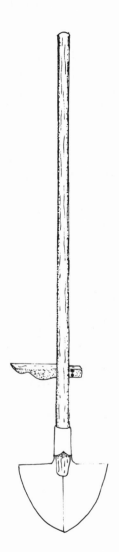

richness could be captured by deep spading and the use of *pollina* (chicken fertilizer allowed to ferment in barrels of water). Of all the smells you can conjure up, none can be worse than the smell of *pollina*. The barrels were kept at the farthest end of the ranch, but you could smell them even upwind.

"No American shovel or fork is worth a damn," complained Nonno. He wrote to a cousin in Italy asking for a hand-wrought iron spade he remembered using as a young man in Bientina. It looked like a plowshare (see illustration) mounted to the end of an extra-long handle, usually a green eucalyptus sapling. The spade could be sunk into the soil about eight inches, but high on the handle, perhaps another ten inches, Nonno inserted a horizontal foot step, which sent the blade deep into the soil when he applied his full weight to it. The long handle allowed maximum leverage, and turned the soil from an extraordinary depth. No one other than Nonno had the strength or technique to dig vegetable plots in this fashion. In late spring, Nonno would dig until he could no longer spear the hardness of the adobe or spit on his hands to grip the handle. To the exposed clumps drying in the sun, he added *pollina*. Not only did the manure enrich the soil, but the wet aplication crumbled the adobe clods into workable loam. The end results were king-size vegetables of the highest quality that sold in Guido's store the minute they went on display.

Friends and relatives who had helped in the construction phase of Redwood City continued to come to help with planting and harvesting. Sometimes they purchased most of the produce, fruit and dressed rabbits, etc., before it ever got to my uncle's store. The lure of Redwood City changed to, "Come and party, and take home groceries."

Nonno built a bocci ball court and horseshoe pits. My uncle Guido paved a portion of the yard near the house for badminton and a single basketball hoop. The surface was terrific for roller skating. At night, this area became the dance floor under overhead lights. Accordions, mandolins, and Nonno's guitar playing provided the music, along with hand-cranked victrolas that played the latest seventy-eights. Though wine and booze were never in short supply, no one ever got rowdy nor incapacitated for the drive back home after gorging themselves on Elisa's breads and pizzas. The barbecue fare ran the gamut of chickens, roasts on a spit, steaks, swordfish, sea bass and albacore tuna, and always, tons of spaghetti and potato salad served from porcelain baby bathtubs that once belonged to Lorraine and me.

It was a time of plenty, youth and carefree innocence, interwoven with hard work that no one resisted. Nonno enjoyed the opportunity to see his family grow and play in a communal environment of love such as I have never seen occur again.

Redwood City invited people to be creative, competitive, generous, and respectful of all there was to be shared. Even Henry Heinrich became an "honorary Italian," enjoying the treat of a German beer supplied just for him. The rest of the week he shared the leftovers and enjoyed his twilight years like a member of the family.

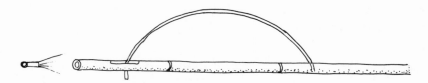

Toy Bamboo Gun

Bamboo Flute

14

The Crossbow and Lute

Nonno was never a meat-and-potatoes man. His tastes favored fish and fowl, for that had been the emphasis of the cuisine in his youth. He often said, "We grew potatoes in Italy to feed the pigs — and beef and pork were for revenue, not consumption." So it wasn't surprising that Nonno devoted a lot of his time in Redwood City to the pursuit of his favorite dish, birds and polenta. My grandmother would cook this delicacy for him whenever birds were available. She created a rich sauce that flavored the polenta (boiled cornmeal) laced with melted Monterey jack cheese.

Blackbirds were the birds of choice, but they swarmed only seasonally in Redwood City, and hunting them was illegal inside the city limits. The remaining options were to shoot local meadow larks, doves, an occasional quail or robins in the winter when they migrated from the north. Though it mattered little to Nonno what birds were sauteed with wine and mushrooms, it mattered a lot to the authorities and game wardens dedicated to protect domestic bird life in the confines of Redwood City. Violators who shot birds could be arrested and fined heavily.

The prohibition made Nonno's longing for his favorite meal all the more alluring, and I was drafted into a life of crime and poaching, because I was a better shot with a BB-gun than he was.

Nonno had attempted shooting his own birds with a .22 rifle—but the size of the shell annihilated any small bird and made it unfit for cooking. Nonno then switched to a .22 scattershot, but the thinned-out shot pattern only wounded the birds, unless he fired from close range. The most successful weapon became a Benjamin compressed-air BB-gun, which fired single shots after "pumping" a barrel piston under the muzzle. The gun was accurate at reasonable distances and a head shot preserved the body of the bird for Nonna's cooking. The disadvantages were the constant need for pumping the gun between shots. You had to press the piston against a solid, flat surface—not always available in the pear orchard. Nonno carried a piece of wood to pump against, but this procedure was noisy and usually scared the birds away.

One Sunday, a county game warden showed up and asked to talk to my father. "Look," he said, "I know your father is shooting birds. I am of Italian descent, and I know he is shooting them for birds and polenta. I don't want to embarrass him by confronting him personally. So I expect you to tell him to knock it off. Your neighbors have complained about the shooting. If I catch anyone shooting birds after this warning, I'll confiscate the weapon and fine you fifty dollars a bird."

My dad thanked the warden for the warning. He knew he meant business. "I'll take care of it," said Dad.

Dad happened to see me first, and he said, "That's it, you guys. That's the end of the BB-gun." To tell the truth, I was relieved. I would do almost anything to please my grandfather—but it bothered me to shoot birds. I kept thinking of orphaned fledglings in their nest. So now I had a reason to decline being an accessory to crime. Selling the threat and warning from the game warden to Nonno, however, was another matter.

"Okay," said Nonno, "no more shooting." Besides, once while pumping the air gun, his finger hit the trigger and he shot a BB into the fleshy part of his left thumb. It took a doctor and stitches to remove the BB. That's when Nonno delegated the hunting to me. But it was only a matter of time, and the yearning for birds and polenta became the "mother of invention."

Nonno set out some of his old fishing gill nets to build a flip-net trap he could spring from behind a blind. By casting bird seed about, close to the folded net on the ground, birds could be lured to feed and scratch, and when enough of them concentrated within the range of the net, Nonno pulled a cord and the net trap would flip over the birds and catch them. A twist of the neck and some quick plucking of feathers generated a dozen birds in short order for polenta. Nonno felt he had not violated the "no more shooting" admonition from the game warden.

My dad was furious with Nonno. "Whoever turned you in for shooting will surely see you net the birds. Don't you come looking to me when you get fined."

This slowed Nonno down a bit. Reluctantly, he dismantled his net trap, but he was far from licked; he still had one trick up his sleeve.

✳ ✳ ✳

The report of the BB-gun or the .22 is what had given Nonno away. What he needed was a "silencer" so that no one could hear he was shooting. He came up with a unique solution: a crossbow that shot not arrows but clay pellets he rolled in his hands and baked in the bread oven. A friend of Nonno's named Pagni knew a little about crossbows. He worked for the Simmons bed works in San Francisco, and had access to a machine shop. He and Nonno devised using a Ford mainspring for the bow and scrap metal parts for a trigger mechanism. This was mounted on a wooden stock. Nonno carved the stock from an arched branch of walnut after a design he remembered using in Italy. As a young man, Nonno hunted birds (illegally) with a crossbow in the forests at night with the aid of a candle lamp held in his teeth. The light was bright enough to reveal birds sleeping on branches. The silence and accuracy of the crossbow permitted an experienced hunter to "pop off" sleeping birds

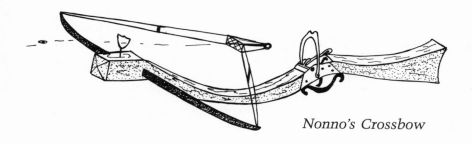

Nonno's Crossbow

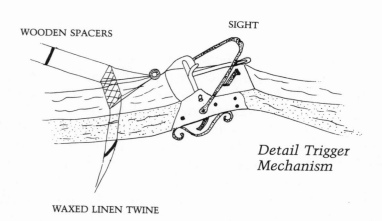

WOODEN SPACERS

SIGHT

Detail Trigger Mechanism

WAXED LINEN TWINE

in succession on a branch without disturbing the next victim.

Pagni and Nonno reveled in the construction of the crossbow as each contributed to the design and workmanship from memory. Sighting the weapon was a fascination for me. They mounted the crossbow in a vise at one end of our workbench. At the opposite end of the bench, some 30 feet away, they hung a burlap target faced with newspaper. When a clay pellet was fired, it perforated a neat, round hole in the paper without penetrating the sack, which absorbed the shot. The clay projectile fell harmlessly to the ground to be used again. A moveable front sight bead on the crossbow kept being moved with every shot until the sight picture from the rear "v" sight was aligned with the hole created by the clay ball in the newspaper. When repeated shots hit the hole every time, the sighting was complete. At this point the crossbow was ready for "William Tell," and yours truly was called upon to try his luck on some birds. Though I lacked the strength to pull the main spring to load the crossbow, I had no trouble firing it. I got so good I could aim at the head of a bird and decapitate it without marring the body for cleaning and cooking. If I happened to miss, the clay pellet would shatter on the branch or obstruction near the bird, and the clay fragments wounded or killed the bird anyway.

I have never known of anyone who went to such measures to ensure a feast of his liking. Even today, I can't eat polenta without recalling how Nonno outsmarted the game warden and frustrated my dad, who washed his hands of the whole affair—but never seemed to refuse his share of birds and polenta.

Nonno seemed to have an endless supply of band-saw blades he obtained from the boatworks at the wharf or from the frozen fish processors who used them to slice swordfish steaks. He made buck saws of every shape and size. Some were no bigger than a foot long for fine work and were used like a coping saw. Some were monsters he would use to slice trunks of walnut or acacia to create planks, which were subsequently planed with his block planes to a smooth glass finish. He never used sandpaper, but rather broken bottle glass, to scrape away a surface to a high-gloss patina.

He made concave chisels for gouging the soles of his scoccoli *(boots) by pounding red-hot iron or steel and then tempering it to razor sharpness. I made his handles for the chisels on my lathe. Many of Nonno's tools have survived to this day and are cherished by my cousins, our children, and me.*

Concave Chisel

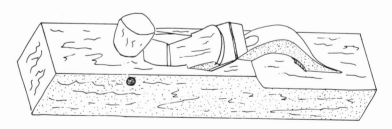

Block Plane

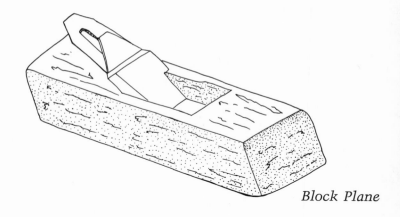

Block Plane

Buck Saw

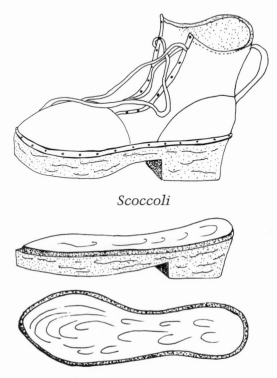

Scoccoli

Wooden soles for Scoccoli

I liked winter in Redwood City because it was too cold and wet to do much outside, so Nonno and I hung around in the workshop inventing projects to keep us busy.

He would be carving *scoccoli*. This traditional winter project involved the carving of wooden soles to replace the customary worn-out leather on conventional boots and shoes. From a pencil foot-tracing for size, he began sawing and carving on wood with a multitude of buck saws and homemade chisels. Either willow or spruce was used to create a pair of sole and heel platforms. On the edges he nailed the tops of the owner's worn-out shoes. A notch running completely around the sole circumference received the leather upper, and a small brass strip secured the leather to the wooden part with small brads. To make the shoe waterproof, Nonno applied hot melted pork fat (he would buy this from the local butcher) to the brass juncture around each shoe. The concave carving on the inside and the slight curl of the sole toward the toes made walking quite comfortable. Surprisingly, one's feet remained warm even in the coldest weather because the shoe stayed dry on the inside, high up from any dampness or puddle through which you might walk. Cleaning mud off of *scoccoli* was a snap—you merely hosed off the shoe.

Anyone who had ever worn Nonno's *scoccoli* had a standing request for another pair. During the year, old shoes that lent themselves to this conversion were saved. The demand prompted my dad, my uncle and me to try our hand at carving, but somehow, though we imitated Nonno's procedure, our versions were never as comfortable as his. The refinement of this skill was most evident in Nonno's hand-made woodblock planes. Not only were they handsome, but they cut effortlessly like razors, creating a uniform curl in whatever wood had to be planed.

To keep Nonno company, I worked on a lathe, which I had built myself, powered by an old washing-machine motor. Nonno loved my endless supply of chisel handles. Nonna had more rolling pins for her pasta making than she knew what to do with. Mostly

Tunes from a Tuscan Guitar

I created woodchips and sawdust, but Nonno and I would admire or criticize each other's projects in good humor, eagerly awaiting the call to lunch or dinner that ended with the entire family adjourning before a roaring fire in the fireplace of the huge living room. Here is where I would be enraptured with Nonno's storytelling. To reciprocate, I would contribute my experiences of my first years at Cal. Since I was the first in my family ever to attend college, my activities were of genuine interest to my grandparents.

They laughed at the high jinks of my fraternity parties, the frustration of studying for finals and my obsession for football games and rallies. This was behavior so foreign to them it was as if I were reciting fiction.

One day, my college life required that I ask Nonno for some help. My fraternity was going to have a "theme" dance and costume party. We had dances periodically and the committee in charge always tried to pick a theme where the girls had to wear the least amount of clothes. Hawaiian and Polynesian themes were popular. Coming up, however, was a pre-scheduled "Renaissance Party." The committee figured on "serving wenches" wearing low-cut blouses. The committee had not figured on the censoring influence of sorority housemothers.

I decided to be a "troubador" à la Chaucer's time. But somehow my ukulele, popular at Hawaiian parties, hardly fit the image and costume I was going to wear. Looking like something between a court jester and Robin Hood, what I needed was a medieval lute. If I could find a lute, I surely could not play it—but ahh, Nonno could help me make one, with four strings tuned like a ukulele, so I could play it with the chord fingering I knew.

After explaining the problem to Nonno, he pulled out a sheet of mahogany door veneer he had been sav-

146

ing and an acacia branch well-suited for a lute handle. We soaked and bent a mahogany strip into the teardrop shape of a lute and then glued a top and back piece to the carved acacia handle, complete with right-angle bend typical of that instrument. Four old guitar strings, tuned to "my dog has fleas," produced a deep, resonant tone. Placing the frets on the handle was a tough problem, I thought. But not for Nonno. His keen ear for music permitted him to space copper wires glued into saw cuttings across the handle of the lute. He placed each fret by ear, sounding the succession of tones on each string.

When we were finished, I could play my ukulele-lute! Nonno accompanied me on his guitar and we laughed at the "prop" we created to go with my costume. Needless to say, I was a hit at the fraternity party playing my repertoire of "Greensleeves," "Five Foot Two, Eyes of Blue"—and "Hail to California" on my ukulele-lute!

15

Christmas Eve

There were many memorable winter evenings in front of that great fireplace. There was no TV in those days, and our entertainment consisted of roasting chestnuts or popcorn or marshmallows—and once green coffee beans, until the drum used for the roasting caught fire. But etched in my memory was an infamous Christmas Eve.

I must back up a bit to Gaspero Cerri who, you may remember, had cemented cobblestones in the early construction years of Redwood City. He was very artistic and was commissioned by a local department store in Antioch, where he lived, to create a Christmas scene as a window decoration. Using a 4-by-8 sheet of plywood as a base, Gaspero built a three-dimensional alpine winter diorama with miniature villages and mountains made from plaster and chicken wire. Little church steeples and village houses lit up. An HBO train traveled in and out of tunnels. Figurines skated on frozen mirrored ponds near snowbanks. Sleds and skiers actually moved to create an animated setting. It won him an award.

The alpine villages surrealistically faded upward into mountain peaks, which transformed into a nativity scene complete with baby Jesus in the stable at Bethlehem, camels and the Wise Men. Atop all of this, a "volcanic" cone mountain received the trunk of a conventional Christmas tree that could spin around on a hidden motorized base.

After several Christmases of use, the display lost

some of its freshness, and just storing this sculpture was a problem for Gaspero. He asked my grandfather if he could store it in the horse barn in Redwood City. Nonno had no objection, and put the display up on the roof rafters. For the Christmas Eve in question, Nonno decided to drag out the decoration into the living room, hoping to delight my cousin Lorraine and me. At this time, we were both on the cusp of still believing in Santa Claus.

The family had settled down in front of sorted stacks of presents, and we were awaiting the arrival of "Santa Claus," who was a neighbor willing to don the costume and play the part.

Nonno's dog, Toby, was asleep by his chair. One of many cats was snoozing under the coffee table. The scene was reminiscent of a Norman Rockwell painting. There was anxious anticipation of the arrival of Santa Claus, because after that, we all got to open our presents.

Suddenly, my grandmother, who was facing the Christmas tree mounted in Gaspero's Christmas scene, said, "Baby Jesus just moved!" No one really reacted; we dismissed a miracle, and we all thought Nonna had a glass of wine too many. But the cat arched its back and was also staring at baby Jesus, and we knew that the cat hadn't had a drink all night. Just as quickly, Toby the dog began to bark and rushed the nativity scene, demolishing most of the alpine villages. What the three had seen was a field mouse boring its way out of the Bethlehem stable. When Toby crushed the chicken wire and plaster mountains, he created a short and some sparks, and what seemed like dozens of mice scampered into the living room!

A nest of them had obviously found refuge in the hollows beneath Gaspero's villages, and the nest had been transported intact into the living room when Nonno helped set up the Christmas tree.

My mother and aunt screamed and climbed upon their chairs, holding their skirts. The cat began chasing mice, and many of them scurried up the drapes. Toby's barking only compounded the problem, and Nonno, my uncle and dad began swatting mice with brooms and fireplace implements or whatever was handy. The room looked like a war zone, at which point Santa Claus arrived, wondering if he had entered a house of maniacs. When a mouse tried to hide in his Santa Claus suit, he became as hysterical as everybody else.

We counted six dead mice, a missing cat, two broken windows and several blood splotches on the floor and furniture. My cousin Lorraine was crying uncontrollably amid the chaos. Each time somebody poked the Christmas scene, more mice ran out and more screams pierced the air.

No Christmas Eve has ever matched the "year of the mice." Nonno loved re-telling the story, a cherished addition to his repertoire that was never surpassed. Each year he would recall the adventure, but never got past the dog barking, because we all would be aching with laughter—and the memory of it still can break me up.

The following summer, Gaspero and his family came to visit, and Gaspero asked Nonno, just out of curiosity, if he still had the display.

Nonno lit his pipe, adjusted his felt hat, and said, "Let me tell you what happened last Christmas!"

*Elisa Bianchi and Ottorino Bianchi on the
occasion of their Golden Anniversary, 1950*

16
Nonno's Trees

It was a Saturday morning before a Cal game at Berkeley when a fraternity brother hollered to me that my mom was on the phone. I instinctively felt something was wrong because my mom rarely called me on campus.

"Hi, Mom. What's up?"

"There's no way to make this easy," she began. "Nonno died last night." She anticipated the stunned silence and went on, "He had a massive heart attack, and we believe he was dead when the ambulance arrived. *Zia* Renata went to Redwood City to be with Nonna, and your father is making arrangements at Valenti Marini."

"Do I have to come to the wake?" I finally asked weakly. I had no desire to view the body. I wanted to remember Nonno as I had known him.

"You most certainly must be there," she scolded. "Your father needs your support."

I went to the Cal game that afternoon, hoping it could distract me, but I can honestly say I can't remember whom Cal played, nor the ending score. The din in Memorial Stadium couldn't erase the flashing scenes in my mind of the happy times I cherished with my grandfather.

The day we hiked up to the Cross in the Woodside hills, and how Nonno tapped the wooden water tank because my cousin and I were dying of thirst. The day he pushed out Lorraine's loose front tooth, and in so doing, knocked out the adjacent one, which wasn't loose at all. She had a double gap smile for a long time. The times he would smoke the hand-carved pipes I insisted on making for him, and how he praised them as wonderful pipes when in reality they smoked hot. The patience with which he'd mend our broken toys. I did not want to believe he was gone, and I had never been sadder in my life.

The mortuary was jammed the first night. Everybody who had ever been to Redwood City showed up. Tappo and the Sicilian fishermen from the wharf arrived en masse. Relatives from both Eureka and Santa Clara were there, as was Pioli from Marin. There was an old Chinese gentleman present no one seemed to know. He didn't converse with anyone, and most people surmised he had just wandered in, or perhaps was a worker for the mortuary. When I was reviewing the guest register, I recognized the name, Chung Wo.

Several months after Nonno died, the family was having dinner at my aunt's house, where my grandmother had already moved.

"I received this strange sympathy card," remarked Nonna. She got up from the dinner table to retrieve it from her bedroom, and returned with two envelopes. The original envelope had no return address but was postmarked Medford, Oregon. It was addressed in a flowing, beautiful, feminine hand to

Mrs. Elisa Bianchi and Family
c/o The Crab Fishermen's Association
San Francisco, Calif.

Mr. Farina had forwarded the card in a cover envelope to my aunt's address, as he knew Nonna was now residing there. The card had no personal message, but the printed word "Sympathy" was superimposed over a graphic sketch of a guitar. The signature was the same handwriting as on the envelope, and it read "A. McCloud."

"Who do we know in Oregon?" asked Nonna. The card was passed around the table. My dad said, "Since it was mailed to the wharf, it must be from some fisherman my father knew in Eureka." I examined the card at some length when it was passed to me. My dad gave me that look I remember as a child when he knew I was telling a lie. "Did Nonno ever talk to you about anybody named McCloud?"

I felt he asked the question like a prosecuting attorney. "No," I replied, as I passed the card to my mother seated to my left. The story of Pinocchio's nose somehow came to mind. I figured Nonno must have had his reasons for not telling that story to anybody but me, and I loved him too much to reveal that confidence to anyone else.

＊ ＊ ＊

Yes, time heals the anguish, but memories remain strong. When I rekindle them, it seems like yesterday Nonno and I were looking at the stars on those clear summer evenings in Redwood City. He'd point out to me the constellations and the signs of the Zodiac, and he would explain how he used them to get home from fishing on late nights when he had to buck the tides.

It might be argued that Nonno never achieved the American dream in terms of financial wealth. He never owned a home nor made a mortgage payment. Though he learned to drive late in life, he never owned a car. But as he struggled in his pursuit of happiness, he endowed his family and progeny, in the wake of his passing, with legacies such as work ethic, optimism, adaptability, love for the arts, music and family—and above all, by example, the importance of a sense of humor.

How grateful I am that quite by chance I now reside in San Mateo. My activities permit me to drive El Camino almost daily through some of the remaining stands of Nonno's trees. On both sides of El Camino between Trousdale on the north and Peninsula Avenue to the south, some of the eucalyptus trees Nonno planted long ago still adorn the highway. Some are a hundred feet or more tall, with trunks six feet in diameter. For me, it is comforting that these trees remain as a living memorial to Nonno, because they remind me how he planted them in an effort to improve his circumstances in a foreign land, and the lifestyle of his family and great-great grandchildren yet unborn. I like to think that Ottorino Bianchi left us the riches of his love—and in that, he succeeded far beyond the American Dream.

It may be just imagination, but when the breeze is right and I choose to listen, I can hear in the rustle of Nonno's trees—faintly, to be sure—the strains of his Tuscan guitar.